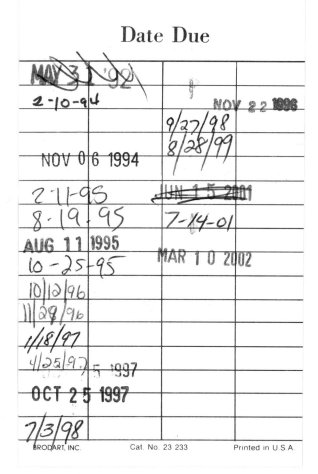

Date Due

MAY 31 '92

2-10-94

NOV 22 1996

9/27/98

8/28/99

NOV 0 6 1994

2-11-95

JUN 1 5 2001

8-19-95

7-14-01

AUG 11 1995

MAR 1 0 2002

10-25-95

10/12/96

11/28/96

1/18/97

4/25/97

5 1997

OCT 25 1997

7/3/98

BRODART, INC.   Cat. No. 23 233   Printed in U.S.A.

FOCUS GROUPS AS QUALITATIVE RESEARCH

DAVID L. MORGAN
Portland State University

Qualitative Research Methods,
Volume 16

SAGE PUBLICATIONS
The Publishers of Professional Social Science
Newbury Park   London   New Delhi

For information address:

SAGE Publications, Inc.
2111 West Hillcrest Drive
Newbury Park, California 91320

SAGE Publications Ltd.
28 Banner Street
London EC1Y 8QE
England

SAGE Publications India Pvt. Ltd.
M-32 Market
Greater Kailash I
New Delhi 110 048 India

Printed in the United States of America
Library of Congress Cataloging-in-Publication Data

Main entry under title:

Morgan, David L.
      Focus groups as qualitative research / David L. Morgan.
          p.   cm. — (Qualitative research methods ; v. 16)
      Bibliography: p.
      ISBN 0-8039-3208-1   ISBN 0-8039-3209-X (pbk.)
      1. Focused group interviewing.   2. Social sciences—Research—
Methodology. I. Title. II. Series.
H61.28.M67 1988
300′.723—dc19   88-11594
                                       CIP

SECOND PRINTING, 1989

When citing a University Paper, please use the proper form. Remember to cite the correct Sage University Paper series title and include the paper number. One of the following formats can be adapted (depending on the style manual used):

(1) KIRK, JEROME and MARC L. MILLER (1986) Reliability and Validity in Qualitative Research. Sage University Paper Series on Qualitative Research Methods, Vol. 1. Beverly Hills, CA: Sage.

or

(2) Kirk, J., & Miller, M. L. (1986). *Reliability and validity in qualitative research* (Sage University Paper Series on Qualitative Research Methods, Vol. 1). Beverly Hills, CA: Sage.

CONTENTS

EDITORS' INTRODUCTION

Social scientists have always been eclectic in their selection of methods and techniques. Even many of their theories are secondhand. They may be Junior League "once-worn garments," rather than Salvation Army "secondhand clothes," but they are from somebody else's closet nevertheless. Models are borrowed from economics, statistics from genetics and agricultural research, and programs from computer scientists. The field of qualitative research has been influenced by notions of reliability and validity borrowed from social survey research operationalism, and has also been shaped powerfully by classic studies that shape and define the nature of "good fieldwork." From time to time, however, the practical world, or what some call the "real world," refines and reshapes a technique of great utility to social scientists. The focus group technique is one of those.

The focus group technique is a tool for studying ideas in group context. The technique has the potential to assist policymaking and policy-driven research, and a long history that extends to Lazarsfeld's Marienthal studies in the thirties. They provide a means for studying one of the cherished propositions of social science: "The whole is greater than the parts." Meanings emerge over time, and are refined. Studies of collective behavior, of experimental cultures formed in the laboratory, and survey research all seek to pin down meaning and to refine its constitutive parts. Much like the Weller/Romney book in this series (*Systematic Data Collection*, Vol. 10), this book, Volume 16 in the Sage Qualitative Research Methods Series, contains a technique for specifying the diversity of meaning. More important, it provides a clear, step-by-step exposition of a means by which to pin down meaning.

—Peter K. Manning
Marc L. Miller
John Van Maanen

PREFACE

I first encountered focus groups when I was looking for a way to generate group discussions that would give me insights into how people approaching middle age thought about heart attacks. I found a great many techniques that used group discussions, but surprisingly few that were actually built around the substantive content of the discussions. My coauthor on that project, Margaret Spanish, and I were about to create our own discussion format when a friend who was completing an MBA suggested that we look into how marketing researchers conducted group interviews. What we found there was remarkably close to what we were trying to create from scratch, and we became focus group researchers.

Since that discovery, I have conducted two major sets of focus groups—the heart attack discussions and a set of interviews with recent widows about factors that affected their bereavement—and have also advised a number of colleagues in setting up their own focus group research. None of this would have been possible without Margie's collaboration, and many of the decisions that we made in adapting marketing approaches to social science research were decisions that we made jointly. We both acknowledge a debt to Pamela G. Smith, who first suggested that we consider focus groups for our research, although she would be quick to point out that her degree is in finance, not marketing.

Between that early point and the present, many others have provided important aid and comfort to this project. Edgar Butler provided support from his bereavement grant (NIA #AG-03857) for a research assistant on the widowhood project, and Diane Vogt provided admirable assistance in conducting those interviews. Despite his own quantitative bent, Robert Hanneman provided what one hopes for from a fellow methodologist: a good listening ear and good judgment. Bob and several of my other colleagues at the University of California, Riverside, are also to be thanked for tolerating the enthusiastic monologues of a researcher who is onto something new. Susan Wladaver-Morgan must also be thanked in this regard, but I owe her a greater debt for her editorial advice on this manucript and everything else I have published. I have learned much from her, as evidenced by the fact that she found only one sentence in this book that was so jargon-ridden that she forced me to fix it by myself. Others whose time and advice deserve thanks include Duane Alwin, Gene Anderson, Benjamin Gottlieb, William Gamson, Linda Kaboolian, Steve Rytina, Eliot R. Smith, and Malcolm Spector. Finally I would like to acknowledge my debt to the late David Street, who gave me an irreplaceable introduction to qualitative methods.

FOCUS GROUPS AS QUALITATIVE RESEARCH

David L. Morgan
Portland State University

1. INTRODUCTION

In a seminar room, a group of returning students, all in their forties, are considering the role of stress in causing heart attacks. There is consensus around the table that stress is indeed important, but what matters even more is how one deals with this stress [Morgan and Spanish, 1985].

In a rural village in Thailand, two groups, one of young men and one of young women, discuss the number of children they want to have and how this has changed since their parents' day. Elsewhere in the same village, groups from the older generation present their views on the same issue [Knodel et al., 1984].

In a church meeting room, a group of widows compare their experiences. One woman complains that other people wanted her to stop grieving in six months, but that it really takes much longer. Another agrees, and says that in some ways the second year is harder than the first [Morgan, 1986].

Each of these examples describes a piece of research using focus groups. As a form of qualitative research, focus groups are basically group interviews, although not in the sense of an alternation between the researcher's questions and the research participants' responses. Instead, the reliance is on interaction within the group, based on topics that are supplied by the researcher, who typically takes the role of a moderator. The fundamental data that focus groups produce are transcripts of the group discussions.

Focus groups had their origins in sociology, although nearly all current applications are in marketing research. Indeed, focus groups are the predominant form of qualitative research in marketing (e.g., Advertising Research Foundation, 1985; Bartos, 1986; Moran, 1986). The development of this technique outside social science approaches to qualitative research is something of a mixed blessing. On the one hand, there is already a substantial literature on focus groups—how to conduct them, what their strengths and weaknesses are, and so on. On the other hand, much of this prior work is based on issues and problems that bear little resemblance to the questions that social scientists usually investigate. Returning the focus group technique to social science research will thus require considerable borrowing and considerable innovation.

Uses for Focus Groups

From a social science point of view, focus groups are useful either as a self-contained means of collecting data or as a supplement to both quantitative and other qualitative methods. The value of combining focus groups with other techniques will receive attention here, but the emphasis will be on the value of self-contained focus groups. This emphasis is necessary because discussions of focus groups in marketing research too often give the impression that focus groups must always be used in conjunction with quantitative methods. If someone were to make this claim against either individual interviews or participant observation, qualitative researchers in the social sciences would have a forceful reply at the ready. Unfortunately, no one has yet made this defense for focus groups.

The typical argument in marketing is that focus groups and other qualitative methods are a useful preliminary or exploratory tool, but that their results must be verified by quantitative work on representative samples. The validity of this argument rests solely on the purposes that one intends for one's research. In marketing, these purposes are largely limited to making accurate projections of future sales for new or revised products; for this purpose representative sampling with standardized survey questionnaires is quite useful. Social science research is not, however, limited to such narrow goals, and there is no a priori reason to assume that focus groups, or any other qualitative techniques, require supplementation or validation with quantitative techniques.

Asserting that focus groups should not be relegated to a preliminary or exploratory role must not, however, blind us to the value of linking focus groups with other forms of data collection, both qualitative and quantitative. In this vein, focus groups are useful for

- orienting oneself to a new field;
- generating hypotheses based on informants' insights;
- evaluating different research sites or study populations;
- developing interview schedules and questionnaires;
- getting participants' interpretations of results from earlier studies.

The important point is to recognize the full potential of focus groups, both as a self-contained means of data collection and as one of several components in a larger research program.

Focus Groups in Historical Perspective

Focus groups are not really new. Within social science, the earliest published work is by Robert Merton and his collaborators, who used focus groups to examine the persuasiveness of wartime propaganda efforts (Merton and Kendall, 1946; Merton et al., 1956; Merton, 1987). Outside of the social sciences, this work was transplanted into marketing research by Paul Lazarsfeld and others. Although his fellow sociologists have emphasized Lazarsfeld's quantitative contributions, marketers have always given equal time to his qualitative work—a balance that was important to Lazarsfeld himself (see Lazarsfeld, 1972), as was his dual involvement in academics and marketing.

Given such auspicious origins, why have focus groups virtually disappeared from the social sciences? One likely reason is that Merton and his colleagues published very little research that used the method they had proposed. For example, in *The Student Physician* (1957), Merton et al. made widespread use of tabulations from survey data and quotations from diaries that the students kept, but only mentioned in passing the fact that they also used focus groups. Meanwhile, work with groups had become closely associated with social psychology, and most of the development of qualitative methods centered on participant observation and individual interviewing. Neglect thus appears to be the basic reason why focus groups never took hold, both by the technique's creators who turned to other pursuits and by its potential users who concentrated on other methods.

To say that social scientists do not practice focus groups per se is not to say that they do not do group interviews; rather, qualitative work with groups has continued at a slow but steady pace. Examples would include the interviews that Hochschild (1983) conducted with groups of stewardesses in *The Managed Heart*, and Gubrium's (1987) observations of a support group in *Old Timers and Alzheimer's*. In the typical case, group interviews are used primarily for convenience—either because groups allow more individuals to be reached at once or because participants are most likely to be located in groups. Perhaps because of this emphasis on simple convenience, group interviewing has never been developed systematically as a research technique in the social sciences.

Focus groups constitute one specific technique within the broader category of group interviewing to collect qualitative data. The hallmark of focus groups is *the explicit use of the group interaction to produce data and insights that would be less accessible without the interaction found in a group*. As already noted, it is in marketing research that focus groups have emerged as a widely used approach to group interviewing—although other fields, such as oral history (Ingersoll and Ingersoll, 1987) have also noted the importance of a more systematic approach to group interviewing. Compared to the refinements that marketers have introduced in their work, group interviews in general, and focus groups in particular, are underdeveloped in the social sciences.

In searching for reasons why focus groups have received a more positive reception in marketing, one factor that stands out is that most of the original work was done in the field of communications research and relied heavily on the use of films and story boards as "stimulus material." Merton and his coworkers argued that this was necessary because it was the discussion of these materials that in fact "focused" the discussion. In reading their manual (Merton et al., 1956), it is often difficult for a social scientist to make the leap to projects that do not revolve around such stimulus materials. This is not the case for marketing researchers, who use a variety of prepared materials in their assessment of how consumers respond to different "concepts" in a marketing strategy. Today, a large proportion of marketing research focus groups still include some presentation of story boards or similar stimulus materials. Thus it may have been nothing more than an initial technical advantage that led focus groups to flourish in marketing research rather than social science research.

Aside from the reliance on externally generated stimulus materials, how do marketing uses of focus groups differ from social science research with group interviews? One limitation on the direct importation of marketing research approaches is that focus groups there became identified with a "psychodynamic" emphasis. Historically, this arose from the fact that technique was brought into marketing at the height of "motivation" and "depth" research. Many early moderators had backgrounds in clinical psychology and one still finds recommendations that moderators should undergo psychotherapy (e.g., Langer, 1978). This approach to focus groups is summarized by Goldman (1962), as coming from a desire to understand one specific form of behavior— purchasing—through a theory emphasizing motivations that the purchaser either remains unaware of ("preconscious") or actively represses ("unconscious"). Like group therapy, group interviewing was supposed to provide the clinically trained observer with new keys to underlying, but fundamentally unobservable, motivations.

A different set of incompatibilities between marketing and social science approaches to focus groups arise from the institutional contexts in which the two forms of research are done. The most notable difference is that marketing applications of focus groups are organized around selling the research to "clients," that is, the people who actually make and sell the product that the marketing agency promotes (Hannah, 1978). The agency sells its research services to the extent that it can convince the client that the results will help the client's bottom line. It is the client who actually pays for the focus groups. Thus the ways that marketers conduct focus groups and the purposes for which they use them are largely determined by the needs of the client.

The fact that marketing applications of focus groups depend on profit and loss must also be taken into account. Many of the day-to-day decisions about how and whether to conduct focus groups are based on the marketing firm's need to show a profit. I will argue next that the uses these agencies make of moderators have as much to do with improving the firm's ability to sell focus group research as they have to do with collecting data. Similarly, if the marketing firm has a considerable investment in its survey research operations, then focus groups may be used largely as a stalking horse to lead clients into more expensive surveys. And the marketing firm may go to great effort to prevent the client from thinking that the supposedly preliminary qualitative research can produce useful results in and of itself.

Of course, social science researchers have their own organizational constraints—for example, a chronic lack of funding, the competing demands of teaching, the responsibility to train students, and so on. And few of us can afford to ignore the opinions of the journal editors and promotion committees who serve as the "clients" for our research. Thus the point of the preceding is not to belittle marketing researchers, but to point out that the structural context in which they have developed and applied focus groups is very different from the kinds of constraints and goals that guide social science research. In adapting focus groups to our purposes, we have much to learn from what has already been accomplished elsewhere, but we also have an opportunity and a responsibility to redevelop these materials. At this time there is very little in the way of received wisdom in the area of social science focus groups.

Overview of the Remainder of this Book

The ultimate goal of this book is to provide the motivated reader with the wherewithal to conduct focus group research. While a slim volume such as this cannot produce "instant experts," it can provide the basis for growth in an area that bears many resemblances to things we already do, but have failed so far to study as a coherent method. As group interviews, focus groups are not so much something new under the sun as a new opportunity to reinvigorate our studies of things that we already do well. Thus a continuing theme of this book is that those of us who become focus group researchers are only occupying a natural niche within the well-defined limits of qualitative research methodology.

The next chapter compares focus groups to the two most common means of gathering qualitative data: individual interviewing and participant observation. Locating the strengths and weaknesses of focus groups is a primary goal of this consideration of them as a qualitative method. Chapter 3 presents a variety of different applications for focus groups as a research technique, both as a self-contained means of collecting data and in combination with other methods. Whether used alone or with other methods, focus groups are treated as something more than a preliminary or exploratory approach to data. Chapter 4 covers the technical aspects involved in planning and running focus groups. That chapter and the next provide a thorough treatment of the practical issues involved in focus groups. Chapter 5 considers a number of ways that research can be designed around the focus groups technique. Although "running a few groups" will undoubtedly remain the most frequent form of focus groups, there are a variety of additional possibilities that go beyond this basic format. The concluding chapter returns to the theme of focus groups as a qualitative method to look at the potential contributions of this new method to social science research, as well as providing suggestions for future reading.

2. FOCUS GROUPS AS A QUALITATIVE METHOD

At present, the two principal means of collecting qualitative data in the social sciences are individual interviews and participant observation in groups. As group interviews, focus groups combine elements of both of these better-known approaches. The intermediate nature of group interviewing means that focus groups not only occupy an easily comprehensible position within the existing set of qualitative methods, but also possess a distinctive identity of their own. On the one hand, focus groups cannot really substitute for the kinds of research that are already done well by either individual interviews or participant observation. On the other hand, focus groups provide access to forms of data that are not obtained easily with either of the other two methods.

In this context, it becomes particularly important to understand the strengths and weaknesses of focus groups, and to do so in comparison to qualitative methods. This pursuit raises questions unique to social science uses of focus groups. Marketing research offers little guidance in this area for the simple reason that there is almost no overlap with the qualitative methods used in the social sciences. There is a clear irony in the fact that focus groups are virtually synonymous with qualitative research in marketing, while they are largely unknown to qualitative researchers outside of marketing. This chapter will begin to redress the imbalance, first by comparing focus groups to participant observation and individual interviews, and then by presenting an overview of the strengths and weaknesses of focus groups as a qualitative method.

Compared to Participant Observation

The main advantage focus groups offer is the opportunity to observe a large amount of interaction on a topic in a limited period of time. The key to this ability is the observer's control over the assembly and running of the focus group sessions. But this control is also the single largest disadvantage of focus groups in comparison to participant observation: they are fundamentally unnatural social settings. Put simply, when there is a premium on the naturalistic ability to observe group behavior and when the opportunity to observe such behavior is readily available, some form of participant observation will be preferred over focus groups.

What are the actual advantages to observing interaction in naturalistic settings? Three major advantages of naturalistic observation are an ability to collect data on a larger range of behaviors, a greater variety of interactions, and a more open discussion of the research topic. By comparison, focus groups are limited to verbal behavior, consist only of interaction in discussion groups, and must be created and managed by the researcher.

First, and most basically, all forms of interviews are based on verbal behavior and consists of self-reported data. If one wants to collect data on other social actions, rather than just the discussion of these activities, then the increased naturalism of participant observation is necessary. Second, even if focus groups do expand the range of behaviors that can be studied in interviews by bringing group interaction into the picture, there are still many interactions that cannot be recreated in focus groups. If the interaction of interest consist of a "discussion," then more naturalistic observation is probably preferable. Finally, because the discussion in focus groups are controlled by the researcher, we can never be sure of how natural the interactions are. If the topic of interest demands relatively uncontaminated statements of the research partici- pants' experiences and perspectives, then participant observation is the closest approximation to this degree of naturalness.

If the great strength of participant observation, in comparison to focus groups, consists of more naturalistic observations, then its comparative weakness is the difficulty of locating and gaining access to settings in which a substantial set of observations can be collected on the topic of interest. A good example is the research that I did on perceptions of heart attack risk factors (Morgan and Spanish, 1985). What we had in mind was a group of people gathered around a lunch table discussing their surprise over a mutual friend's heart attack, an image that we labeled, "Oh my God, not Harry!" Certainly such interaction occurs, but where could we find the opportunity to observe it? By conducting focus groups we admittedly had to trade off the immediacy and emotion of a naturally occurring episode such as the lunch conversation, but this was not really a loss, as we could not "trade off" what we never had access to in the first place.

There is a more subtle implication to the value of focus groups in research areas in which a dense set of observations is difficult to locate: we tend to do participant observation in settings in which there is something immediately available to observe. For example, there are excellent studies of patients recovering from heart attacks, using the hospital as a point of access, and starting with observations in the intensive care unit (e.g., Speedling, 1982). One reason that topics like social roles and formal organizations are so frequently studied by participant observation is that they are structurally well suited to the method. Of course the fundamental importance of roles and organizations to social theory is also a factor. Still, more social psychological topics, such as attitudes and cognitions, appear to be slighted, not because they are less important, but because they are less well suited to the method.

Because both focus groups and participant observation share an overlapping interest in group interaction, there are many topics for which it would be possible to design a study using either of them. In this case, there is a trade-off between the naturalness of observations in a field setting and the ability to collect a concentrated set of interactions in a very short span of time via focus groups. This is not the sort of choice that can be made on strictly technical grounds. The different value attached to the advantages and disadvantages of the two methods will depend upon the research topic itself, the background and interests of the researcher, and the nature of the ultimate audience for the research.

Does this mean that there is an element of competition between participant observation and focus groups? I think not: instead, I would foresee a developing division of labor between the two. For example, I have already suggested that focus groups are better suited to topics of attitudes and cognitions, while participant observation is superior for studies of roles and organizations. Even if there turn out to be many topics for which either technique is potentially appropriate, I predict that there will still be clear grounds for preferring one or the other.

Compared to Individual Interviews

The comparative strength of focus groups as an interview technique clearly lies in the ability to observe interaction on a topic. This is the main reason that marketers give for preferring them over individual interviews. Thus Bellenger et al. (1976) note that the give-and-take of interaction leads to relatively spontaneous responses from participants as well as producing a fairly high level of participant involvement. Similarly, Levy (1979) states that hearing how participants respond to each other gives insight not just into their natural vocabulary on a topic, but also when they are willing to challenge others and how they respond to such challenges. Although more balanced comparisons of group and individual interviews can be found in the marketing literature (e.g., Greenbaum, 1987), this approach is relatively rare in that field.

Fern (1982, 1983) has argued that such marketing claims have created a semimagical appeal for groups—asserting the superiority of group interviews, but never really comparing them to individual interviews. In a controlled experiment, Fern (1982) showed that groups did not produce significantly more or better ideas than an equivalent number of individual interviews. Thus, if a large volume of ideas is the research goal, it would be preferable to conduct individual interviews without fear of loss of quality. As Fern notes, however, other claims about the supposed superiority of group interaction remain untested—and in some cases are so vague as to be untestable.

Clearly, a piece of social psychological research that had interaction as its topic would be a good candidate for focus group interviewing, but there are other circumstances in which groups offer an advantage as well. One advantage of group interviewing is that the participants' interaction among themselves replaces their interaction with the interviewer, leading to a greater emphasis on participants' points of view. As will be discussed in Chapter 4, it is possible to conduct self-managed focus groups in which there is no preconstructed interview guideline or questionnaire, effectively removing the researcher's perspective from the interaction. This advantage should not, however, be overemphasized, as both individual and group interviews can be arranged on a continuum from more structured, researcher-controlled formats to less structured, participant-dominated formats. While individual interviewing is also interaction, the key point is that focus groups offer a stronger mechanism for placing the control over this interaction in the hands of the participants rather than the researcher.

Another advantage to group interviewing is that exploratory research requires less preparation. The advantage again derives from the ability to conduct the research with less in the way of a prepared interview. Of course the price one pays for this approach is relatively chaotic data collection, with little comparability from group to group. One way to resolve this is to conduct a small number of such groups, perhaps as few as two, and then use the results as the bases for the creation of a more structured interview guide that could either be pursued in more groups or serve as the basis for individual interviews.

The ability to rely on group interaction, as opposed to interviewer instruction, does have a price of its own. In particular, the generally higher level of researcher control over interaction in individual interviewing translates into a comparative advantage in managing what data are actually collected. This advantage is clear in comparison to the just-noted chaos of self-managed groups, but it is still easier to pursue new leads or skip unwanted material in one-on-one interaction than in even the most structured of group interviews.

One supposed advantage to group interviews is that they are cheaper than individual interviews, but is this really so? The answer depends on whether the researcher pays participants, hires a professional moderator, or rents a specialized taping facility. In individual interviewing, participants are usually volunteers who are interviewed by the researcher in some mutually convenient location. By comparison, focus groups are certainly much more elaborate, but this may not necessarily involve additional expenses: some individual interviewing projects require payments for a variety of services, while some focus groups are done on an entirely self-supported basis.

A more clear-cut comparison is the amount of time involved: The same number of participants can be interviewed in much less time in a group format and with a further savings in analysis time because fewer transcripts are required. Of course this also produces proportionately less data than interviews with the same number of individuals. When Fern compared the number of ideas generated in focus groups and in an equivalent number of interviews, groups produced roughly 70% as many ideas as individuals (not counting duplicate ideas in either the real groups or equivalent samples of individuals). Whether this is considered a substantial savings of time or a substantial loss of data will depend on the nature of the research problem and the resources that are available.

From this discussion, it should be apparent that there is more room for competition between focus groups and individual interviewing than was the case in the comparison to participant observation, if only because both are interview methods. My personal point of view is that it is better to recognize this potential problem from the start and begin to resolve it by a program of cooperative research that employs both techniques within the same research project.

The potential for cooperation can be illustrated with the question of whether interviews produce different data, depending on whether they are conducted on an individual or group basis. The answer is certain to be "yes" for an unknown number of topics. The answer to the further question of which method is to be preferred in what circumstances is anything but clear cut. If we begin with focus groups, there is an irreducible uncertainty about what the participants might say in private. Yet, if we begin with individual interviews, there is no way to know what individuals might say if others were present. On some topics, groups may inhibit discussion; on others, they may lead to collective flights of fantasy. On some topics, individuals may be more honest with an outside interviewer, and on others, with their peers. What we need to do is to begin cross-validating by applying the two modes of interviewing to the same topics. The question of which method is better in which circumstances is essentially an empirical one, so it will take research using both techniques to provide an answer. Only then will we begin to define the areas for which individual or group interviews are to be preferred.

Strengths and Weaknesses

Pulling together the various strands from these discussions reveals a pattern of strengths and weaknesses for focus groups as a technique for collecting qualitative data. Focus groups are no different from any other method, qualitative or quantitative, in this regard—there are some cases in which they are to be preferred and others in which to be avoided. This summary will argue that the strengths and weaknesses are intertwined: Anything that a technique does notably well is done, at least partially, at the expense of other things that can only be done poorly. Thus the strengths and weaknesses of focus groups will be presented in pairs—a corresponding weakness for each area of strength.

The practical strength of focus groups lies in the fact that they are comparatively easy to conduct. In many circumstances, the research can be done relatively cheaply and quickly. This is not to say that *all* focus groups research is simple—as we shall see, it is possible to design projects of considerable complexity—but when time and/or money are essential considerations, it is often possible to design focus group research when other methods would be prohibitive.

The price one pays for the ease of conducting focus groups was emphasized in the comparison to participant observation: focus groups are not based in natural settings. As such, there is always some residual uncertainty about the accuracy of what the participants say. This translates into a preference for more natural settings when these are readily available or crucial to the research.

Procedurally, the strength of focus groups lies in their ability to explore topics and generate hypotheses. When the researcher is relatively new to an area, or puts a priority on not repeating the received wisdom in a field, focus groups have much to offer. The fact that group interviews can produce useful data with relatively little direct input from the researcher may be a distinct advantage, especially in comparison to other interviewing techniques.

The corresponding weakness, as noted in the comparison to individual interviews, is that the researcher has less control over the data that is generated. The degree of control is not an all-or-nothing issue, but focus groups can never match the potential of individual interviews in this regard. This translates into a preference for more controlled approaches when there are a clear set of predefined issues or a strong need to maintain strict comparability across separate interviews.

Substantively, the strength of focus groups comes from the opportunity to collect data from group interaction. The point is not, of course, to tape-record just any interaction, but interaction that concentrates on topics of interest to the researcher. When all goes well, focusing the group discussion on a single topic brings forth material that would not come out in either the participants' own casual conversations or in response to the researcher's preconceived questions.

The problem with relying on interaction in groups is never knowing whether or not it would mirror individual behavior. Indeed, there are whole lines of research in social psychology that are dedicated to investigating the ways that individual behavior differs from group behavior—for example, individual decision making versus group influence (Janis, 1982). The point here is not so much whether one is interested in groups or individuals, as that individual behavior is subject to group influence. But whenever observing individuals in groups will distort what one is studying, methods other than focus groups should be preferred.

Summarizing these strengths, what focus groups do best is produce an opportunity to collect data from groups discussing topics of interest to the researcher. In part, this strength reverses some of the other two weaknesses. Because the researcher defines the discussion topics, focus groups are more controlled than participant observation, and, because of the participant-defined nature of group interaction, the focus group setting is less controlled than individual interviewing. In other words, focus groups occupy a position that is intermediate between the two most frequently used means of collecting qualitative data.

Morgan and Spanish (1984) noted that this compromise between the comparative strengths and weaknesses of the other two techniques bears a resemblance to Howard Becker's two dimensions for classifying qualitative data (Becker, 1958). On the first dimension, Becker distinguishes between data that is volunteered by informants and data that is requested by the researcher. The second dimensions distinguishes whether the data is publicly presented in the presence of other informants or shared with the researcher alone. The naturalistic advantage of participant observation is that it produces volunteered information in groups, while individual interviews emphasize the control available through private contact between the researcher and the participant.

In the case of focus groups, the typical presence of the researcher as a moderator in a focused discussion of a preselected topic means that the data lean toward the researcher-directed and publicly stated poles of the continuum. As a compromise between the strengths and weaknesses of the other two techniques, focus groups are not as strong as either within their specialized domains. But the respective weaknesses of the other techniques tend to lock each of them into their narrowly defined domains, while focus groups can easily operate across traditional boundaries. This flexibility may be the greatest strength of focus groups.

None of this is meant to overstate the strengths of focus groups: given their potential weaknesses, there are many cases in which focus groups would not be the preferred method. The frequent goal of focus groups is to conduct a group discussion that resembles a lively conservation among friends or neighbors, and most of the problems come from topics that fail to meet this goal. If the participants are not sufficiently involved in the discussion, the group moderator will have to question them closely to get the desired materials, and individual interviews thus might be more appropriate. Similarly, if the participants do not know enough about a topic, the researcher may collect only scattered instances of the desired material, and participant observation in an appropriate site might produce more data.

A different set of problems arises if the topic is highly controversial, or if there is a real potential for disagreement among the participants. On the one hand, if the participants do not feel comfortable about revealing their opinions on a topic in a group setting, then individual interviews may be more effective. On the other hand, if bringing together different participants with different opinions will produce conflict in the group, then it would be preferable to do participant observation in a setting that they do share successfully—if no such setting exists, then it may be asking the impossible to create it in a focus group!

But one should not get the impression that topics for focus groups are limited to bland discussions about common topics. As an example of how to handle controversial topics, there is Knodel's work (e.g., Knodel et al., 1984) on family planning decisions, and as an example of how to provoke discussion about topics that participants seldom think about, there is my own work on heart attacks (Morgan and Spanish, 1985). One way to determine whether or not a topic will work in a focus group setting is to pretest. In this case, the "tone" of the group discussions provides clues about the appropriateness of focus groups; Levy (1979) suggests noting how easily and openly the topic is discussed and the range of emotions that appears. Unfortunately, at this point in the development of social science focus groups, we know relatively little about the range of practical topics. Only further experience will provide better insights into this issue.

Summing Up

The issues raised in this chapter really respond to two separate questions: First, when are focus groups a workable alternative for a given research project? Second, given that they are at least possible, when are they actually to be preferred over other qualitative methods?

The simplest test of whether focus groups are appropriate for a research project is to ask how actively and easily participants would discuss the topic of interest. At this point, social scientists have done little to explore or develop focus groups, so I would recommend being relatively liberal in assessing their workability for a given project. If there are barriers to active and easy interaction, this may be overcome by some of the discussion techniques described in later chapters. In such a case, one would, in all honesty, be well advised to build back-up data collection strategies into the research design. But if some researchers who use focus groups are disappointed by the results, it is vital that they find a forum for saying so. At this point, the field of social science focus groups cannot grow without a few public accounts of cases in which focus groups were tried and found inappropriate.

Saying that focus groups are a *workable* option for a research project is not at all the same as saying that they are the best way to gather the data for that project. One goal of this chapter has been the forthright recognition that there are many circumstances in which a different form of qualitative research will produce data that are more appropriate to the researcher's goals. In the same spirit, I have also claimed that there are other circumstances in which focus groups would in fact be preferable to either participant observation or individual interviews. The implication of this argument is that we may look forward to a further division of labor among qualitative techniques, which will improve our ability to match our methods to our research questions.

3. THE USES OF FOCUS GROUPS

This chapter will present focus groups as both a self-contained research method and a technique that can be used in conjunction with other methods. As a self-contained method, focus groups can be used either to explore new research areas or to examine well-known research questions from the research participants' own perspective. In combination with other methods, focus groups can be used either as preliminary research to prepare for specific issues in a larger project, or as follow-up research to clarify findings in the other data.

A somewhat different issue is raised by the assumption, firmly rooted in marketing, that focus groups are largely limited to preliminary or exploratory research, whether they are self-contained or explicitly part of a larger project. In this view, focus groups are not a means of answering research questions. Templeton (1987: 192) dismisses the claim that focus groups can lead to better questions as "very faint praise indeed." But this is precisely what exploratory or preliminary research is supposed to accomplish; as such it is a definite virtue of focus groups. The danger comes from the assumption that focus groups must be limited to such preliminary and exploratory purposes. To counteract this assumption, this chapter will emphasize the ability of focus groups not only to generate but to answer research questions.

Whether one is using focus groups alone or in combination, whether one seeks questions or answers, the goal in using focus groups is to get closer to participants' understandings of the researcher's topic of interest. This is frequently stated as finding out their attitudes and opinions, but I find this summary too limiting. Instead, I emphasize learning about participants' experiences and perspectives. One reason to prefer experiences is that even self-reported behavior is more useful as data than are opinions that have an unknown basis in behavior. I also prefer experiences because a discussion of them produces a livelier group dynamic—people are more than happy to compare their different experiences, while they might be reluctant to challenge someone else's opinion. I prefer perspective because, while attitudes and opinions are typically treated as small, discrete parts of a participant's thinking, a perspective implies a broader basis for specific attitudes and opinions. Focus groups are useful when it comes to investigating *what* participants think, but they excel at uncovering *why* participants think as they do.

Self-Contained Focus Groups

The key distinguishing feature of a self-contained focus group is that the results of the research can stand on their own. Note that this does not deny that the data could also be used as part of a larger project; rather, it asserts that no such further data collection is necessary before reporting the results from the focus group research itself. Two common ways in which self-contained focus groups combine with other sources of data are when they contribute to the ongoing research program of a single author, or when they become part of a larger subfield. As such, they are part of a larger effort to "triangulate" different forms of data collection on the same topic (Denzin, 1978; Fielding and Fielding, 1986), and their independent, self-contained nature is a crucial feature of their ability to contribute to triangulation. This can be illustrated by two examples of self-contained focus groups that are also part of larger research programs.

Knodel and his co-workers (Knodel et al., 1987; Pramualratana et al., 1985) conducted two sets of focus groups with members of the older and the younger generation in Thailand to explore differences in their fertility practices. The results stand alone as an explanation of how the two generations perceive and explain the differences in their choices with regard to family size, even though, as the authors point out, a different explanation might emerge from the additional analysis of censuses and the further collection of demographic survey data. In that case, further research would "validate" not the focus group results, but rather the perceptions of the participants.

In my work on widowhood and bereavement (Morgan, forthcoming), I examined findings from surveys that families had little impact on the recovery from bereavement, even though widows said their relationships with family were important. In focus groups in which widows discussed what made it easier or harder for them, I found that the importance of family made widows more likely to both endure negative relationships with family and provide many services to family members, despite their own grieving. This account of the limitations in family relationships could be tested with survey data, but the data stand alone as a summary of how these widows recounted the ways that others made their experience easier or harder.

These two examples demonstrate how participants' discussions of their experiences and perspectives serve as the fundamental data in self-contained focus group research. One obvious approach to such data is to examine the content and frequency of different attitudes. Thus Knodel's research team built part of their analysis around the comparison of attitudes among different regions and religious groups, while part of my analysis is based on a content analysis that counts how often family and friends were mentioned in positive or negative contexts.

These examples also demonstrate the emphasis that focus groups place on the manifest content of the group discussions. There is typically little attention to either the microdynamics of the interaction process or the contextual constraints of the focus group setting (cf. Goffman, 1981). To be sure, marketers train moderators to pay attention to the nonverbal aspects of the interaction, but this is nothing like the careful attention to turn taking, eye contact, pauses in interaction, patterns of speech, and so on, that could go into an analysis of these conversations. The present discussion will continue to emphasize the substantive content of focus groups, although future efforts to explore other dimensions of the interaction in them are both relatively straightforward and welcome.

As already noted, the direct reporting of experiences and perspectives does not make full use of the insights that focus groups provide. Going beyond summaries of attitudes takes us into the thought processes that produce these statements of opinion. There are a great many ways to express the goals of this kind of research. For example, Pramualratana et al. (1985: 209) speak of finding the norms that underlie decisions about age at marriage, and consider the advantages and disadvantages of using focus groups to reveal "basic values." My own approach emphasizes the social cognitions that are involved in any discussion of topics that are of mutual interest to the participants.

The basic building blocks in this cognitive process can be referred to either as schemas (typically in psychology and anthropology) or as perspectives (typically in sociology), but regardless of the field of origin, the emphasis is on a summary way of representing the perceived world (see Morgan and Spanish, 1987, for a comparison of schemas and perspectives). From this point of view, what focus groups do is treat these perceptions and their representations as the basis for a discussion among a set of participants whose schemas and perspectives may be either subtly or wildly different. While it would be an oversimplification to say that cognitive processes are unmeasurable (see Taylor and Fiske, 1981), the argument for a social cognitive view of focus groups is that cognitive processes are revealed through interaction in ways that it would not be possible to observe otherwise.

It is important to distinguish this approach to cognitive issues from the more psychodynamic approach that characterizes many marketing applications of focus groups. The key difference is that marketers are selectively fixed on the psychological factors affecting only one form of social behavior: purchasing. According to Templeton (1987: 71), "The things that focus group researchers principally seek to learn about are things that [participants] rarely think about very concentratedly: buying, brand-choice usage, and product attitudes, for instance. These things are negligibly important to them as ordinary citizens in the real world." Compare this to the two examples of focus groups given previously, family planning and widowhood. What we as social scientists are most likely to study are events and issues that are manifestly important to our participants. And, while we are unlikely to ignore completely the issues of motivation that are so important to marketers, our cognitive questions concentrate on how people express their normally private perceptions of these events and issues.

Based on our research into the perception of heart attack risk factors, Margaret Spanish and I (Morgan, 1986; Morgan and Spanish, 1984, 1985) provide a description of the cognitive processes that are observable in focus groups. The basic idea is that an emerging discussion in a focus group is in many ways analogous to the process of schema or perspective formation in an individual. The group begins with relative uncertainty about the extent to which participants share a common set of perceptions on the discussion topic. As more members of the group present their experiences and perspectives on the topic, they typically find some common means for representing areas in which they both agree and disagree; they may ultimately come to some further realizations about the sources for their various levels of agreement and disagreement. Compared to survey research, in which interviewers typically encounter problems when they ask about issues about which the participant does not have a well-formed opinion, this example shows that focus groups are a good way to observe the process of opinion formation.

From a cognitive point of view, the process of creating and using summary representations of perceptions is basic to all of human experience. As Agar (1986) points out, this process of forming and modifying schemas in the search for some ultimate resolution among different experiences and perceptions is also what researchers do in trying to understand their data. What Spanish and I are advocating is the use of focus groups as means to observe this process. The research that we conducted on perceptions of heart attack risk factors illustrates four aspects of the group discussion that can serve as the basis for observing and interpreting cognitive processes in self-contained focus groups.

First, we would advocate paying attention to the difference between what participants find interesting and what they find important. A lengthy discussion of a topic is a good indication that participants find it interesting, but not necessarily that they think it is important. The single topic that these returning students found most interesting was stress, and a large part of the reason was the lack of any broadly shared summary of what it was, how it operated, or what to do about it. By contrast, there were nearly as many mentions of cigarette smoking, but almost no detailed discussion of this topic, because nearly all participants rapidly discovered that they shared the same perspective on what the ill effects of smoking were and how they operated. Hereditary factors would constitute an intermediate case: this topic nearly always sparked a controversy between those who thought it was crucial and those who thought it was trivial. In some groups this difference in perspectives led to an extended debate, in others it led to a search for risk factors that were agreed upon.

Second, differences in perspectives are also revealed through how questions get asked and answered. A notable example of this in the heart attack focus groups came from requests for further information following a story about someone who had had a heart attack. These questions often carried the implication that something had been left out of the story—that the questioner's schematic summary of the story required information that the teller had not found either interesting or important enough to include. In providing the answer, the teller often admitted that including this information did lead to a new perspective on why the person had a heart attack. These questions were being used to bridge the differing information requirements of different perspectives. Seen in this light, questions can be more than just requests for clarification, they may provide insights into thought processes.

Third, both of the previous two aspects of focus group discussions implicitly raise issues about how participants agree and disagree in the group. Discovering when perspectives are shared or when one person's schematic summary of an experience is not sufficient for another to evaluate the same event is something that can happen only in interaction. As a technique, focus groups emphasize keeping the participants discussing a subject until their points of agreement and disagreement become apparent. This often means that participants become consciously aware of their own perspectives when confronted with an active disagreement or an explicit attempt to reach consensus. In the heart attack discussions, some of the more interesting discussions were attempts to resolve differences between those who believed that heart attacks were controllable through individual behavior (e.g., smoking, diet, and exercise) and those who believed that they were beyond personal control (e.g., due to genetic inheritance, or ultimately traceable to the pace of modern life).

Fourth, attempts to resolve differences and build consensus are only one of several mechanisms whereby participants build comprehensive models to explain their various experiences with a topic. Such collective attempts to create or expand a perspective are inherently limited to groups. Certainly not every one of the heart attack groups attempted to build a comprehensive model, and still fewer succeeded. Part of this difficulty reflected the nature of the topic: understanding the causes of heart attacks ultimately calls for expert knowledge that these people did not possess. A comparison to the focus groups I conducted on widowhood (Morgan, forthcoming) is instructive. In those groups, there were two important elements of general consensus: that each individual's experiences were unique and that what each person needed was acceptance by others of her need to grieve. This flexible shared perspective proved useful for discussing the specifics of individual cases on a topic for which expert knowledge is of less immediate importance.

The value of observing these four aspects of the group discussion process is not limited to the cognitive approach described here. Stripped of their baggage of schema and perspective, interest versus importance, question asking and answering, the handling of agreements and disagreements, and the building of comprehensive models would still be worthy of the researcher's attention in any set of self-contained focus groups. The reason is that these examples make use of group interaction as a strategy for investigating the participants' responses to the research topic. Given that the discussions among the participants are the primary data that self-contained focus groups produce, it makes obvious good sense to use them as the basis for observation and interpretation, no matter what one's own theoretical perspective is.

As the various examples should make clear, what one observes in a self-contained focus group and how one interprets it are largely functions of the topic under examination. The specifics of how to conduct self-contained focus groups are thus equally variable. Portions of this issue will be taken up in each of the succeeding chapters: technical information on how to plan for and conduct them in chapters four and five, and general suggestions for research designs involving self-contained focus groups in chapter 6.

Linking Focus Groups and Individual Interviewing

Chapter 2 has already noted the points of contact between individual and group interviewing and put forth the broad argument for combining the two within research projects as a way to explore the relative strengths and weaknesses of each method. This discussion will not emphasize issues of cross-validation so much as the ways that focus groups can enhance projects that are largely based on individual interviews. This will be the pattern in each of the next sections: Beginning with the presumption that another technique has already been selected as the primary means of data gathering, the presentation of focus groups will emphasize the ways that they can add to the larger program of research.

The single most important way that focus groups can contribute to a project built around individual interviews is in devising the interview schedules. The idea is to use a small number of exploratory focus groups in the very early stages of the research to guide the later construction of the interview questions. This is obviously most useful when the topic or study population has not been extensively studied in the past or when the researcher is new to an established area. Initial focus groups are also of value, however, in ensuring that well-studied topics are being researched from the participants' perspective and not just through a set of disciplinary filters and blinders. One promising, but as yet untried, technique would be to get the individual informants to respond to actual transcript segments in their interviews.

A different use for focus groups would be to use their time advantage relative to individual interviews to compare different groups of participants. Thus, in a project that needed to select the most useful comparison from among several population groups, a preliminary round of focus groups would provide a basis for selecting groups for the more detailed interviews. This would be especially useful if one set of individual interviews was already completed and the goal was to select among several groups for a comparison to the existing data.

A final way to triangulate focus groups with individual interviews is to conduct the groups as a follow-up to the interviews. This would allow the researcher to explore issues that came up only during the analysis of the interviews. It would also be a way to clarify areas in which there seemed to be a number of different viewpoints in the individual responses. In an inversion of the earlier suggestion, it could be interesting to get the group response to quoted segments from individual interviews.

As these suggestions show, focus groups need not be limited to a preliminary rehearsal for the collection of individual interviews. The same point will be made with each of the other methods to be discussed next. Rather, there are reasons to conduct focus groups before and after individual interviews, and even circumstances in which one would want to alternate back and forth between the two methods. The important point here is that the goal of triangulation is to strengthen the total research project, regardless of which method is the primary means of data collection.

Linking Focus Groups and Participant Observation

The principal things that focus groups have to offer to a project based on participant observation is a concentrated insight into participants' thinking on a topic. Although this can be of value at any point in the history of a project involving participant observation, it can be especially useful at the beginning of a new project. This is particularly true when one is entering a field site that differs sharply from the researcher's prior experience. In this case, the focus groups provide an initial exposure to the typical experiences and perspectives of those one is about to observe. Given the well-known problems of access and the sensitivity of entering a new field site, it would, in many circumstances, be advisable to conduct these preliminary groups with participants drawn from similar locations other than the research setting itself.

Often the selection of a site for participant observation is anything but straightforward, and focus groups can help in this regard as well. As with individual interviews, focus groups can be conducted with participants from each of several possible field settings, to provide a basis for deciding among them. In this case, the comparative focus groups are most useful for deciding among alternative types of settings, rather than among specific geographical locations. Comparing potential field settings to each other is especially useful in projects that use multiple field sites. Glaser and Strauss's (1967) constant comparative method is one notable approach to designing a larger participant observation project around the comparison of multiple field sites. In this format, one completes a set of analyses at one site, and then searches for a theoretically motivated second site that will provide the most informative comparison as to what is already known. Focus groups in a number of different settings would provide a good insight into the kind of second study that would provide the most useful comparison.

Focus groups would also be useful as a means of implementing the constant comparative method itself. Once the base set of observations was complete, the comparisons could be made via a set of follow-up focus groups with participants from theoretically selected subgroups. Such a substitute obviously lacks the richness of direct observation in natural settings, but it has the advantage of feasibility. Given the amount of time and effort that is necessary to conduct participant observation in even a single location, it is not surprising that the constant comparative method is most often honored in the breach. Implementing the constant comparative method through focus groups does have its limitations, but these may be more than balanced by its practicality.

So far, the suggested uses of focus groups in combination with participant observation have concentrated on groups that are conducted outside the field site itself. One circumstance in which it would be desirable to draw the participants from the study site is at the end of the study, as a way to test the researcher's understandings. By presenting areas of researcher interest to the participants as topics in a focus group discussion, it is possible to get direct insights into their own feelings in the matter. Of course it is also important to bear in mind that these discussions provide only self-report data; the participants may not have accurately analyzed the patterns in their own behavior or they may have good reason for refraining from public statements about every aspect of this behavior. In other words, discrepancies between the data from focus groups and participant observation do not inherently favor the participants' own statements in the focus groups. Further, when such discrepancies do occur, they themselves may be an important form of data.

Linking Focus Groups and Surveys

Although several important sources on how to conduct survey research recommend using focus groups to construct questionnaires (e.g., Converse and Presser, 1986; Rossi et al., 1983), there is little published evidence that this advice has actually been put into practice. In the case of social science surveys, the absence of explicit descriptions of how to triangulate focus groups and surveys is probably a result of the relative rarity of this combination, but no such excuse exists for marketing, in which focus groups are routinely matched with survey research. The present treatment cannot offer the depth that would be necessary for complete coverage of this subject. What I offer instead is an extended description of how focus groups can contribute to survey research projects, in hopes that their expanded use by social science survey practitioners will generate the baseline studies that are necessary for further growth in this area.

In their early history, surveys relied more on their potential respondents in the initial development of the questionnaire—for example, Thurstone's informants acted not only as judges of the proposed questions, but as sources of the original item pool (Thurstone and Chave, 1929). As the number of available survey items has increased dramatically, so has the tendency to replicate existing items from other surveys. Aside from saving the work involved in developing new items, preexisting items typically carry some evidence of reliability and validity with them. Unfortunately, the evidence for validity may be quite weak, often consisting of nothing more than a nonzero correlation with a criterion measure, that is itself of unknown validity. Further, as we shall see next, even this evidence speaks only to what a set of items contains, and not to what it omits.

To the extent that the borrowed items were generated in an "armchair" fashion, rather than through actual contact with the potential survey participants, their use may constitute a thoroughly reliable replication of an essentially invalid measure. Unfortunately, we have little basis for judging the magnitude of this problem. We are rapidly reaching a point at which most general population surveys consist entirely of items that have never been validated outside the confines of other surveys.

The most obvious way that focus groups can assist in item and scale construction is through providing evidence of how the respondents typically talk about the topic in question, a goal that is often summarized as learning their language on a topic. A more important use for preliminary focus groups is to ensure that the researcher has as complete a picture of participants' thinking as possible. This is especially important for making sure that issues that might have been ignored in an outsider's inventory of the topic are included. An example comes from survey research that used focus groups to prepare for a study on the household division of labor in dual income families. One unanticipated factor that the researchers uncovered was that couples make allowances at home to compensate for the circumstance in which one of them had a job that is either more physically exhausting or dirtier than the other's. The point here is not so much the value of including one specific item in an area that admittedly applies to only a subset of households, but the cost of omitting it for those couples when it does play a substantial role in their household division of labor.

Such omissions constitute a form of specification error, such that the relations among the variables that are measured would differ if this variable were taken into account instead of ignored. Although this class of error has no effect on simple descriptive statistics, it can be a severe problem in multivariate analyses. In the present example, ignoring how dirty or exhausting a job was would probably have little effect in those households in which both wage-earners held white-collar jobs, but the omission could produce a substantial bias in blue-collar households. The all too obvious danger is that such omissions are not random, given the unavoidable class and occupational differences between survey researchers and many of their respondents.

Focus groups are also useful beyond the preliminary or exploratory phases of survey research. In particular, they can augment the pretesting that is necessary to evaluate the survey instrument. If the researchers are relatively unfamiliar with a given topic or if issues of language are a particular problem, then it would be advisable to hold a group discussion of the proposed items in crucial sections of the questionnaire, prior to pretesting in the field. In addition, Knodel and Pramualratana (1984) suggest that one advantage of focus groups is that it is much easier to detect if participants fail to understand a question as the researcher intended it. Pretesting with focus groups would not only locate such problems but allow an immediate exploration of how to correct them.

When a full pretest version of the questionnaire is ready, then a different kind of feedback comes from administering the questionnaire to a set of participants and listening to their reactions in a focus group. According to a recent news report, even the IRS is now pretesting its forms via focus groups! According to Axelrod (1975a), marketing research clients are sometimes taken aback when they listen to "flesh and blood consumers." Survey researchers may be similarly surprised by what a group of their respondents say about a questionnaire. But Axelrod also warns against being overwhelmed by the power or novelty of the experience: don't let one chance remark from a single respondent kill a good idea. The goal is to learn from the experience, to let it guide one's work, not determine it.

At the later stages of a survey, when the data are in and the analysis begins, focus groups can serve as a follow-up data collection, pursuing "exploratory" aspects of the analysis. This is especially important when the results are puzzling to the researchers. Too often the tendency is to throw every possible variable into the analysis, then retreat to our armchairs and speculate about what might have created the results. Asking the participants themselves is a better strategy. Did they understand and respond to the questions in the way the researchers intended? Did they consider factors that the researchers failed to question them about? Can they give a straightforward basis for their responses that can be tested as a hypothesis? Even when the surveys available are secondary data, focus groups can provide further insights into respondents' thinking. A recent book by Knodel et al. (1987) provides an excellent illustration of the ways that focus groups can be combined with existing survey data.

An illustration of the value of focus groups for explaining unantici-pated results comes from my work on widowhood. In an otherwise excellent analysis of exchange among family members in widowhood, Rook (1987) was puzzled by the fact that widows were happier when they received more instrumental support than they gave to their children (exchange theory would predict a preference for more balanced relationships). Rook attempted to resolve this outcome with a rather elaborate and ad hoc explanation from attribution theory about the greater legitimacy of receiving aid among older family members. My observations suggest a different source for the imbalance: problems among those widows who were providing more assistance to their children. Several of the widows expressed difficulties in providing support to their children for problems such as illness, divorce, and unemployment while they themselves were still grieving. They did not question the need to provide this support, because it fit within their norms about family obligations, but they did note the toll that it took on them. Rather than abstract issues of over- versus underreward, what seemed to be at issue was how widows cope with the very real needs of others, which can not be ignored just because of bereavement. (In fairness to Rook, she does avoid the simplistic exchange theory derivation that widows can cope with their bereavement by helping others, although this assumption is common in other segments of the widowhood literature.)

As these various examples show, focus groups have a considerable potential for contributing to survey research. If some of these suggestions have been more critical than those for other methods, it is largely because survey research has been so successful at establishing itself as a self-sufficient source of social science data. In the absence of adequate triangulation, however, such self-sufficiency may become inbreeding. Given the importance of surveys to social science research, it makes sense not only to make use of every advantage that they offer, but also to take advantage of what other methods have to offer. Survey researchers have often noted the potential value of combining their work with focus groups, and it is now time—and past time—to move forward in this regard.

Linking Focus Groups and Experiments

Although there is now almost no recognition of the potential value of focus groups in experiments, this was, in fact, one of the key applications for group interviews in the research program of Merton et al. (1946, 1956). In their introductory chapter, they note four uses that they made of focus groups in combination with their communication experiments: specifying the effective stimulus, interpreting discrepancies between anticipated and actual effects, interpreting the ways in which subgroups differ from the effects prevailing in the larger population, and interpreting the process involved in the actual production of experimentally induced effects.

Using preliminary focus groups to define "manipulations" of independent variables and measures of dependent variables is analogous to developing questions in interviewing techniques. By exploring the topic of interest with the targeted subjects of the research, it is possible to operationalize the theory in a way that is meaningful to the participants. Such improvements typically come under the heading of increasing external validity, a perennial issue in experimental research. What is less frequently realized is that this same process also increases the chance of designing a successful experiment. This occurs because focus groups can help the researcher in the selection of more powerful manipulations for the independent variable and more sensitive measures for the response variables. As with surveys, focus groups can be used for this purpose both before and during other forms of pretesting—and if pretest subjects can be run in batches, then there is an excellent opportunity for a focus group immediately following the pretest.

Following the completion of an experiment, focus groups provide an effective substitute for armchair speculation in explaining any anomalous results. The tendency for experimental researchers to feel qualified to explain their own failed predictions stems in part from their assumed familiarity with the population they typically study: students. Even when the study is done on the proverbial college sophomore, rather than some less frequently contacted group, there is no substitute for exploring the research outcomes with the participants who in fact generated them. Indeed, most experimental recruitment procedures are remarkably well-suited for recontacting the original experimental subjects and bringing them together for a follow-up discussion.

A different kind of follow-up is necessary when the experiment generally worked as planned, but not equally well for all participants. In this case, focus groups with the different subgroups may assist both in clarifying current results and determining the direction of future experiments. To locate subgroups, post hoc comparisons can show that results would be either significantly stronger if some subgroups were eliminated or nonexistent without a strong response in one or two subgroups. When known groupings for such comparisons do not exist, one can still identify outliers and use those with statistically deviant response patterns as the basis for conducting follow-up groups.

The final advantage that Merton et al. cite in combining focus groups and experiments is the improved interpretation of how experimentally induced effects actually operate. As with follow-ups using focus groups with other methods, the goal is to compare the researcher's interpretation of events to the interpretations of the participants. Merton et al. provide examples of how interviews with participants can lead to the recognition of previously ignored experimental factors, and even to the development of whole new lines of research.

Summing Up

As noted at the outset of this chapter, the value of linking focus groups to other methods should not detract from their potential as a primary method of data collection. Nor should their role in triangulation be limited to purely preliminary exploration. One way to make these points is to draw attention to a whole series of possible research designs that are missing from this chapter: Those in which focus groups serve as the primary means of data collection with supplementation from individual interviews, participant observation, surveys, or experiments. Such combinations are at least as useful as those discussed here, but the relative newness of focus groups in the social sciences means that we shall have to wait for the development of triangulated research that uses focus groups as a point of departure.

A final point should be made to connect the material in this and the previous chapter: Other qualitative methods could be used to make these linkages, and may in some circumstances be superior to focus groups for this purpose. While focus groups may have some advantages in this regard, it is best not to overstate them. The argument for triangulation is essentially a plea for the mutual relevancy of all research methods, rather than the superiority of any one technique. In this spirit, the value of any new method can be increased only by explicitly linking it to existing methods.

4. PLANNING FOR FOCUS GROUPS

This chapter addresses the planning that must be done prior to doing focus groups. Both this and the next chapter, on how to conduct and analyze focus groups, will have more of a "nuts and bolts" emphasis. Such practicalities are an important aspect of any research technique, and focus groups do not differ greatly from other qualitative methods of data collection in this regard. In particular, the framework for the next two chapters is based on Kirk and Miller's (1986) general description of the four phases of qualitative research, planning, observation, analysis, and reporting.

Of the four phases in the life of a research project, this presentation will devote one entire chapter to the planning phase. I emphasize planning because this is the area in which focus groups depart most from standard practices in other qualitative methods. The fact that they are *group* interviews is the source of most of these planning needs. Once the choices surrounding the format of the group interview are made, the subsequent observation, analysis, and reporting phases will pose issues that are already familiar to experienced qualitative researchers.

Before Starting

The two most obvious factors affecting the ability to plan are budget and time constraints, but there are other, less obvious constraints. One such constraint is whether the project is self-contained or linked to other data collection. As noted in the previous chapter, focus groups are especially valuable in combination with other techniques; this chapter will, however, concentrate largely on self-contained focus groups. The reason is that self-contained focus groups are the most basic version of the technique, and any usage in combination with other data collection strategies is basically a variation on the self-contained focus group.

Political and ethical issues raise another set of preliminary issues. In many respects, the issues with regard to focus groups are similar to those raised in all qualitative research (Punch, 1986). Invasion of privacy issues are particularly acute, given that taping is the primary means of data collection. Actual audio and visual presentation of tapes are relatively rare in the social sciences, but they can be very tempting in the case of focus groups—no amount of accuracy in transcription will ever substitute for the excitement of actually listening to an emotional exchange among participants; video tapes can be even more seductive. Thus one must decide up-front who will hear (see) the tapes. My advice would be to limit this to the research staff: unless you know from the beginning that public presentation of the tapes will be an integral part of your research, it is best to avoid this issue altogether.

One set of ethical issues unique to focus groups arise from the fact that the material that research participants share with the researcher is inherently shared with other participants as well. This raises serious invasion of privacy issues and effectively limits the kinds of topics that the researcher can pursue. Such limitations are actually practical as well as ethical: it is not a productive use of focus groups to ask people to discuss topics about which they are not used to expressing their thoughts in public, or to ask them to do so with discussion partners with whom they are not comfortable. Certainly ethical issues go well beyond what people are comfortable with or articulate about, but often enough practical barriers to free-flowing focus group discussions will arise even before invasion of privacy issues do. In other words, most focus groups that constitute invasion of privacy are also a waste of the researcher's time. But note that this argument does not necessarily apply to groups of self-acknowledged deviants, especially if they are members of deviant subcultures in which the informal equivalent of focus group discussions occur. In this case, one needs to exercise the usual protection of participants, with the added assurance that all discussion participants truly are a part of the shared milieu.

Turning to budget as a constraint on planning, one guideline is that marketing researchers typically charge clients over $2,000 for groups from the general population and this may double when working with specialized groups of more-difficult-to-recruit participants. If the research is being subcontracted to a marketing firm, this is what it will cost you. If you are doing it yourself, it will probably cost substantially less. The most obvious savings comes from the elimination of the need to make a profit. Less obvious savings come from the fact that conducting work within a research framework is more straightforward than the client-management mode that operates in much of marketing research— there will be no need to arrange for a catered dinner behind a one-way mirror for the clients' representatives who will be observing your groups.

Major cost factors can include: salaries to moderators, travel to research sites, rental of research sites, payments to participants, and tape production and transcribing. Most of these costs are essentially fixed by the circumstances of the research, but there is a substantial possible savings if the researcher has the time and skills necessary to perform the moderator function. This is especially true if the only alternative is hiring someone with a marketing background, as the costs assigned to such people are a major component of the charges that marketing firms make to their clients. While it is true that these are highly trained individuals, it is also true that marketing firms often assign very high costs to these individuals as a way to "assure" clients that they are getting high quality research.

If social science budget constraints are usually less severe than in marketing research, time constraints are likely to be more severe. The reason is that marketing firms are typically geared up to produce summary reports to clients within a one- or two-month time span, but social science operations lack the staff to do this and would be unlikely to settle for the kind of report this produces. An experienced team undoubtedly could produce a summary report in as short a time as one month. This may well be sufficient when focus groups serve only as a preliminary to the major data collection, but a serious, self-contained focus group project will take considerably longer.

In the planning phase itself, decisions for a set of focus groups typically require at least two weeks, and more if the research team is inexperienced with the method. In the observation phase, recruitment of participants may be quite time-consuming when specialized populations or experimental designs are used. Even though the groups themselves take only a few hours to conduct, two a day, or even five a week would be a killing pace without either a very large staff or considerable reliance on outside services. Finally, in terms of analysis and reporting, transcript typing is slow, and transcript analysis is very time-consuming. Depending on the number of groups, the availability of the participants, and the kind of analysis intended for the transcripts, count on a project taking between three and six months (longer if the staff divide their time between the research and other commitments).

From the beginning, it is important to have realistic expectations, not just with regard to budget and time, but also in terms of the total amount of investigator effort that is necessary to produce the desired data. This is hardly a new problem, but because of the relative novelty of focus groups in social science research, it deserves attention. The reputation that focus groups have in some marketing circles as a "quick and easy" technique is due to the very limited function to which they have too often been relegated: preliminary explorations to set the stage for "real" research. When pursued as a full-fledged research technique in its own right, focus group research demands the same attention to detail as any other means of data collection. As is always the case, the quality of the data depends on the quality of the preparation: Careful planning cannot guarantee insightful results, but a cavalier approach to the design and execution of the research is almost certain to produce poor results.

Determining the Number of Groups

The number of groups is the first planning issue to be discussed because the reader needs to get in the habit of thinking of the group as the fundamental unit of analysis in focus group research. This is true not only in a statistical sense, but also in terms of practicality: duration of the group is usually fixed at one to two hours, and only a relatively narrow range of group sizes is practical, so the number of groups is the primary dimension of variability. One immediate result of this emphasis is that the size and structure of the research team should reflect the number of groups that it will be conducting. Conducting many groups almost ensures the need for a larger research staff, the only other alternative being to extend the data collection and analysis over a longer period of time.

Your research goals will determine your choice with regard to the number of groups you conduct. Marketing researchers provide a clear example here, varying the number of groups according to whether the additional discussions are producing new ideas. According to Calder (1977), if the moderator can clearly anticipate what will be said next in a group, then the research is done; this usually takes 3 or 4 groups. Thus research that is exploratory in nature or simply aimed at "getting someone's perspective" will probably take only a few groups with relatively high degree of moderator-imposed structure, but if the goal is detailed content analysis with relatively unstructured groups, then six to eight (or more) groups will be necessary. (The issue of moderator involvement in the structure of the focus group will be considered in some detail later in this chapter.)

One important determinant of the number of groups is the number of different population subgroups required. The more homogeneous your groups are in terms of both background and role-based perspectives, the fewer you need. But one group is never enough: you may be observing little more than the dynamics of that unique set of participants. Even if you run only two and they are highly similar, you are on much safer ground. Further, as discussed later, if there are several distinct population segments in the groups that you are studying, you may want or need to run separate groups in each, e.g., groups composed entirely of men and run separately from groups composed entirely of women. Running a minimum of two groups in each distinct segment will obviously increase the total number of groups.

A different set of issues are raised by how dispersed the participants are and how flexible the research team is. If relatively few of the participants live in a given area, then there may be little choice but to run more groups, each smaller in size, at a number of different sites. Alternatively, if the research team is relatively unable to travel, you may have to settle for fewer groups, based on the number who can be recruited at your location.

In general, the goal is to do only as many groups as are required to provide an adequate answer to the research question, because there are few economies of scale to doing many groups. Each additional group adds directly to cost and time factors. Still, there is a danger to limiting one's planning to running a bare minimum number of groups, as this can make you vulnerable when groups fail to run or are so unusual as to be of dubious utility. The best advice is to determine a target number of groups in the planning stage, but to have a flexible alternative available if more groups are needed.

Determining the Size of Groups

There are both practical and substantive considerations in selecting the size of groups. On the practical side, there are some economies of scale to running larger groups, if only because it takes fewer groups to hear from the same number of participants. On the substantive side, the dynamics of discussions in smaller groups are likely to be different from those in larger groups. The usual conclusion is to use "moderate sized" groups, which is somewhere between 6 and 10, depending on what source you read (in marketing, the currently favored range appears to be 6 to 8; several years ago it was 8 to 10).

Substantively, small groups demand a greater contribution for each individual participant. This may mean only a larger total volume of comments from each, but this need to make a larger personal contribution often produces a dynamic of higher involvement in the life of the group. When the researcher desires a clear sense of each participant's reaction to a topic, small groups are more likely to satisfy this goal. In larger groups, there is the possibility of "social loafing" (cf. Latane et al., 1979), that is, each individual participates less because the group as a whole can carry the discussion. But if the researcher has no reason to hear from each and every participant, what does it matter how evenly spread the discussion is? If the goals of the research are purely exploratory, then running a few large groups may well provide a quick and clean solution. This is especially likely to be the case if the focus groups serve as a preliminary to a different mode of primary data collection.

Turning to more practical matters, small groups run the risk of being both less productive and more costly. Smaller focus groups have problems with productivity because they are so sensitive to the dynamics among the individual participants. In particular, the functioning of the group as a whole can easily be disrupted by friendship pairs, "experts," or uncooperative participants. The high cost of running many small groups is largely a problem when the analyst runs more such groups to ensure a larger total number of participants. If the design calls for a fixed number of groups, regardless of size, then cost is less of an issue. As noted, the costs involved in running more groups involve the researcher team's time and travel in the data collection, and a larger number of transcripts to deal with in coding and analysis.

Larger groups have practical problems of their own. The more participants, the more difficult it is to manage their discussion. Large groups typically require a higher level of moderator involvement, and it takes an experienced moderator to control them without engaging in continual efforts at discipline. As discussed later, such high levels of moderator involvement are not always desirable. A different set of problems involve the difficulties in finding facilities that can accommodate larger groups. One particular danger is that discussions in large groups can break up into small conversations among neighbors around the table, which implies a loss of data because such conversations are very difficult to tape.

Combining both practical and substantive considerations, it appears that four is the smallest size for a focus group, and the upper boundary—although less clear-cut—appears to be around 12. This is not to say that group interviews of some kind cannot be done with smaller or larger groups, but it would be best not to call them focus groups. Whatever size is selected, it is important to overrecruit in order to cover for no-shows. The common rule of thumb is to overrecruit by 20%, although the actual extent of overrecruitment depends on where the groups are conducted, who the participants are, whether they are being paid for their participation, and how vital the size range is for the overall design of the research.

Determining the Source of Participants

In selecting participants, the issue is sample bias, not generalizability: 40 or so participants are never going to be representative of a large population. This is especially important when one's research goal is not to test hypotheses but to learn about others' experiences and perspectives. Using focus groups to learn about the full range of experiences and perspectives in a broad population can be a fool's errand. Indeed, there is often no reason to believe that a randomly sampled group holds a shared perspective on your topic. A typical solution, given the small size of focus group samples, is to work with theoretically chosen subgroups from the total population. It is good advice to "concentrate on those population segments that are going to provide the most meaningful information" (Axelrod, 1975b: 10).

The result is that focus groups are often conducted with systematically selected samples: either all the participants come from one limited source, or major groups are consciously omitted from the data collection. Such bias is a problem only if you ignore it, that is, if you interpret what you hear in the focus groups as representing a full spectrum of experiences and opinions. This strategy often leads to the use of a research design based on selected comparisons; for example, if gender differences are a major issue, then you might run separate groups of men and women and compare their discussions. To continue the example, if class differences are not a major issue, then your comparisons may be facilitated by using participants who are all blue-collar or all upper-middle class, but you will need to be forthright in recognizing and reporting on this sample bias.

The recruitment of participants can require a great deal of effort, unless you really are working with general community population and can "take people off the street." If you need specific categories of participants, plan to devote a real effort to locating them. Telephone screening interviews are one useful approach. This involves calling either a random sample or a predetermined list and using a very short questionnaire to see if there is anyone in the household who both fits your category and is interested in participating. Such screening is more than just a mechanism for locating participants: "Purity" is important if you are recruiting narrowly defined groups. Even if only one of the participants fails to share some crucial characteristic, the discussion can get totally off track. If this is a severe problem in a specific research design, then a further screening questionnaire, administered just before the group discussion, can serve as a final filtering mechanism. Be warned, however, that screening questionnaires do run the risk of alerting participants to your areas of interest in advance—or at least creating such expectations, whether they are accurate or not.

When working with highly specialized subgroups, recruitment procedures have to be equally specialized. In particular, it may be necessary to use substantial cash incentives to recruit top-level executives or others with unusual expertise. Payments of $50 to $100 per person per session are not unusual, but if the research has an external sponsor that is meaningful to the participants, this might substitute for a cash incentive. You may also find that marketers have already established a "going price" for a set of participants; for example, because sales of prescription drugs depend on physicians, they are a popular target of focus groups for pharmaceutical companies, and expect to be paid handsomely for their participation. One general strategy for dealing with difficulties in the recruitment of highly specialized groups is to conduct informant interviews with a few representatives of the category—even qualitative researchers occasionally need to be reminded of the value of getting their participants' perspectives on a problem.

A perennial problem in determining the source of participants is the decision between mixing different categories of participants and running separate groups for each category. The problem arises because of the need to maintain a reasonable amount of homogeneity within groups in order to foster discussion. The best general advice is that participants should really have something to say about the topic and they should feel comfortable saying it to each other. Would these participants normally discuss topic in day-to-day interaction? Participants must feel able to talk to each other, and wide gaps in social background or life-style can defeat this. Note, however, that the goal is homogeneity in background, not homogeneity in attitudes. If all the participants share virtually identical perspectives on a topic, then this can lead to a flat, unproductive discussion.

The most common background variables that are considered in running mixed versus separate groups are sex, race, age, and social class. Whether the sexes interact differently in mixed groups is an ongoing research question (Thorne and Henley, 1975), but if the issues raised by a given topic are not gender-linked, then even real differences in styles of discussion may not affect the information that is conveyed. Similar remarks apply to race, although, given the rather selective integration of American society, there are more topics through which racial differences may become an issue during group discussions. Older and younger participants may also have difficulty communicating with each other, either because they have different experiences with a topic or because similar experiences are filtered through different age-based perspectives. Class differences reflect a general segregation of interaction in our society, so that even when there are few overt class differences in the experiences of participants, they may be too uncomfortable discussing personal experiences in each other's presence. This last illustrates a more general point: it is not the actual differences among participants, but whether they perceive each other to be different, that determines their willingness to discuss a topic together.

I can illustrate these points from my research on widowhood, in which the participants were largely women in their sixties and seventies, though one group had two male participants and another group contained a very young widow. For both of these cases, there was a moderate disruption in the flow of the discussion, as the other participants went out of their way to be solicitous to the "outsiders" in their group. Yet all of the groups were quite mixed with regard to social class, which had had little noticeable impact because these widows believed that their bereavement created a fundamental similarity among them that overwhelmed the differences in their backgrounds. In other words, their shared beliefs determined what made another's experience similar or different.

The choice between mixing and separating categories of participants also occurs when they occupy different roles with regard to a topic. Thus the differences between husbands and wives in a discussion of household decision making is not just a difference between men and women. This issue is particularly common in organizations, in which individuals in various positions have routine patterns of what they do and do not discuss together. In such cases, you must ask what you would be likely to learn by creating contact among different groups, if it is indeed rare for this topic. The typical decision is to avoid mixing categories because the probability is high that the discussion will degenerate in either of two ways: a refusal to share experiences and opinions across categories, or uncontrollable conflict.

Running separate groups because of background or role-based differences has the cost of requiring more groups, because it takes a certain minimum number of groups within each category to observe the range of response to your topic. If you run separate groups, it is best to think in terms of about four groups per type. In other words, each separate category becomes its own focus group study. This strategy can be expanded to include also a direct comparison between discussions within separate categories and discussions that combine the categories of participants. Note, however, that with two categories this means three sets of focus groups; with more categories it can become very unwieldy.

An alternate way to answer the question of mixing or separating is to try some pretest groups each way: if these do not differ, there is little reason to use separate groups.

A final decision with regard to recruitment involves using strangers versus allowing friends to participate together. As a general rule, it is better to work with strangers, unless friendship either is an important element of the research topic or the topic is something that would normally be discussed only among friends. Although friends converse easily, this is often a result of their ability to rely on the kind of taken-for-granted assumptions that are exactly what the researcher is trying to investigate. This problem is even more severe when the assumptions include invisible boundaries around the subjects that friends have tacitly agreed not to discuss among themselves. Using friends also presents practical problems: It is difficult to recruit friends who form a single group, and mixing friendship groups produces complicated group dynamics that may defeat even a skilled moderator. Eliminating friends is typically accomplished by screening during recruitment, but this process is anything but foolproof. Fortunately, it is seldom fatal if a group recruited as strangers in fact contains one friendship pair.

Determining the Level of Moderator Involvement

The level of moderator involvement is usually treated as a continuum: at the low end, moderators play only a small role in the ongoing group discussion and attempt to keep their comments as nondirective as possible; at the high end, moderators control both the set of topics that are discussed and the dynamics of the group discussion. Within marketing research there are occasionally acrimonious debates over the value of one extreme or the other, although the trend historically has been toward higher levels of moderator involvement. Early marketing researchers tended to favor nondirective styles as a way of getting at psychodynamics—revealing more "depth" (e.g., Goldman, 1962). The more recent preference for high moderator involvement pays less attention to psychodynamic theory and concentrates instead on using moderators to get the most useful material from the participants (e.g., Wells, 1974).

This emphasis on a high level of moderator involvement is a good example of the constraints imposed by pursuing research within a marketing context. In the typical marketing research project, the moderator represents the research group to the client and often presents the results to the client (e.g., Welch, 1985). Thus the emphasis on a prominent role for the moderator within the actual groups can have as much to do with the moderator's role in managing the client (who is, after all, paying for the research) as it does with the data to be collected. This need for the moderator to "perform" is reinforced both by the emphasis on videotaped presentations of results to clients and by the common practice of having the client "sit in" and observe at least one ongoing group from behind a one-way mirror.

My own favored approach is a form of highly nondirective focus groups that I call "self-managed groups," which will be discussed later. Rather than advocate this or any other style of focus group, however, the discussion here will be highly pragmatic: researchers must decide what they want their interview materials to produce and then make decisions about moderator involvement in line with these goals. I would not hesitate to advise someone with different goals from mine to use a high-moderator involvement format, *if* that was the appropriate way to produce the data that would meet their research goals.

Low levels of moderator involvement are important for goals that emphasize exploratory research. Are the basic issues well known? Does existing knowledge come from participants' perspectives, or is it based on researcher-imposed agendas? If the goal is to learn something new from participants, then it is best to let them speak for themselves. Low levels of involvement are also important when your goals include doing a full-scale content analysis; otherwise your results will reflect what the moderator, not the participants, thought was interesting or important. Alternatively, high levels of involvement are more appropriate when there is a strong, externally generated agenda. Examples include: addressing issues for use in another research setting; comparing the thinking of a new set of participants with what has been found in a previous set of groups; or, providing answers to a set of sharply drawn research questions.

If research goals do not provide a definitive answer for a specific project, then attention shifts to the pros and cons of each form of involvement. The most obvious problem for high involvement is that a biased moderator will produce data that reproduces these biases, whether they are the personal biases of the moderator or the larger presuppositions in the research team. Kennedy (1976) also notes that moderators have a bias toward consistency: early sessions produce a set of research-based expectations, and moderators may avoid leading later groups into discussions that invalidate what has already been achieved. Note also that all of these problems will be magnified in smaller groups, where there is more intensive contact between the moderator and each participant.

On the pro side, a highly involved moderator has the ability to cut off unproductive discussion and to probe what the researcher wants to know more about, so long as this is not carried to the extreme of imposing the moderator's own sense of what is interesting or important. The highly involved moderator is thus walking a tightrope between what Bellenger et al. (1976) term *understanding empathy* and *disciplined detachment*. High involvement also has the ability to ensure that a desired set of topics are covered, although this should not occur at the expense of letting participants raise their own points of view. As Templeton (1987: 45) notes, it is important to direct the discussion without "putting words into panelists' mouths." Finally, high moderator involvement allows for adjustments in the discussion, depending on the level of homogeneity among the participants: putting groups of very different participants at ease and sparking discussion in groups where everyone already shares an implicit perspective.

For low levels of moderator involvement, the biggest plus is the ability to assess participants' own interests. This can be important even when there is an externally generated research agenda, because it shows whether participants naturally organize their discussions around the same things that researchers do. For example, in my work on heart attacks (Morgan and Spanish, 1985) I wanted to find out if participants used the concept of risk factors (they do), while Gubrium (1987) used his participant observation of Alzheimer's support groups to find out if caregivers shared researchers' emphasis on the "burdens" of caregiving (they do not). A different advantage of low moderator involvement is that participants can bring up controversial topics that would threaten moderator rapport, although this may occur at the expense of the moderator's ability to maintain rapport among the group members themselves.

A major disadvantage of low moderator involvement is that these groups are relatively disorganized in their content. They are thus more difficult to analyze than the well-ordered discussions of specific topic areas produced by highly involved moderators. This is especially true in large groups. Another problem is that some topics may never come up. Rather than simply presume that such a topic is of no importance or interest to the participants, it may be the case that they would be more willing to discuss it if a moderator cued them to do so. A failure to discuss an explicitly introduced topic is stronger evidence of a lack of interest than a mere failure to raise it.

Much of this discussion has a "Yes, but . . ." flavor that emphasizes the very real limitations of a rigid pursuit of either high or low moderator involvement as a goal in and of itself. Unfortunately, many marketing researchers do take such a rigid approach with regard to advocating high levels of involvement. To redress this imbalance, I will describe a specific technique for minimizing moderator involvement: self-managed groups. (Advice on how to conduct research with high levels of moderator involvement can be found in Higginbotham and Cox, 1979.)

All too many marketing research descriptions make it sound as if group discussion would collapse without the active presence of a moderator, but remember, the services of the moderator are the main thing that agencies are selling, so self-interest may prevent them from seriously exploring self-managed groups. The most frequent reason they give for high involvement is to control interaction in the group: getting irrelevant discussion back on the track, restarting discussion when the group runs dry, ensuring that "groupthink" doesn't stifle opinions that differ from the majority, cutting off overly dominant participants, engaging overly reticent participants, and so on. But most of these problems can be handled through self-managed groups.

Here are some explicit techniques for getting the group to solve problems in interaction through self-management. Each of these themes would be introduced at the beginning of the session by the moderator, who would then retire to a separate table to take notes. Here are sample instructions, but you do not need to drum them into the participants—if the group is larger than four or five, you can safely count on someone's remembering and applying an instruction.

Legitimate the members' right to manage the discussion by creating a self-fulfilling prophecy: "If you tend to get off the track, someone will usually pull the group back to [your topic]—we'll jump in if we have to, but usually one of you takes care of that for us."

Cue them on handling common problems: "If the group runs out of things to say, just remember that what we're interested in is [your topic] and we want to hear as many different points of view about this as possible. So what usually happens is that someone will think of something that hasn't come up yet and then that story will restart the discussion."

Emphasize that you want as many different points of view as possible: "If your experience is a little different, then that is exactly what we want to hear. Often someone says, 'I guess my experience is different from everyone else's . . .' and then they find out that the same things have happened to other people too, but no one else would have mentioned it if someone didn't start the ball rolling."

Get them to use questions to direct the flow of interaction: "If someone hasn't really joined in, or you seem to be hearing from the same people all the time, try asking a question to someone who hasn't spoken as much. Everyone will say a little bit about themselves in the first part of the discussion, and you can use this information to ask them a question later."

Emphasize hearing about their experiences—not everyone is willing to state or defend an opinion, but most people are willing to tell their stories: "We want to hear as many stories as possible. Even if you think your experience is just like everyone else's, don't just say, 'I agree.' We want you to tell us your story, because there's always something unique in each person's own experiences."

Emphasize that all experiences are equally important to you: "We need to hear as many different things from as many of you as time allows. There really aren't right or wrong answers in this area—if there were, we'd go to experts and they'd tell us the answers. Instead, we're here to learn from your experiences."

A different solution to choosing between high and low levels of moderator involvement is to plan for a design that combines the two. One way to accomplish this is to begin with a set of self-managed groups and use the data they produce to develop and interview guide for a second set of more highly moderated groups. Another approach is to run most of each group as self-managed, and then follow-up with more specific questions, for example, "One thing that we're specifically interested in hearing more about is. . . ." But note that if you do content analysis on designs that combine high and low levels of moderator involvement, be sure to tabulate the two sets of data separately, as different mechanisms have produced the relative frequency with which topics were mentioned in each.

Implicit in all of this is that a single moderator will be conducting all of the sessions. Although this is preferable for purposes of comparability, it is all but impossible in larger projects. Multiple moderators obviously have few effects on self-managed groups, but they require an additional element of planning at higher levels of moderator involvement. In this situation, it is useful to designate one person as the senior moderator and have this person lead the first one or two groups, with the other moderators in attendance. Thereafter, it is useful if the senior moderator attends the first sessions conducted by each of the other moderators, and for the moderators to meet as a group from time to time. This format is especially appropriate in the common circumstance where the senior moderator is training the others as new moderators.

One final lesson can be learned from your planning with regard to the level of moderator involvement: your preference can signal the possibility that you should be using another qualitative technique. Thus if you are planning on a highly structured format, then you ought to consider doing individual interviews instead. Similarly, if you are planning on a highly unstructured format, then you ought to ask if you could do participant observation instead. Just as it is important to question the reasons for your preference on level of moderator involvement, it is also useful to back up and ask why you have selected focus groups as a technique for gathering qualitative data.

Summing Up

Clearly there are a great many issues to be considered in planning for focus groups. This chapter has only touched on a set of general issues that are likely to affect nearly all focus groups; any specific research project will confront many more issues than this. In addition, it would be unwise to give the impression that planning really is a discrete stage in the research project. Planning is not something that is over and done by a given point, with a totally new set of concerns waiting to replace it. Many of the issues covered in the next chapter will also require planning. The strength of focus groups as a relatively easy and quick form of research does not eliminate the need for planning. Indeed, this chapter should have made it painfully obvious that the only way one can take advantage of the flexibility of focus groups is through a diligent effort at prior planning!

5. CONDUCTING AND ANALYZING FOCUS GROUPS

This chapter takes up the questions of how to do focus groups and what to do with the data they produce. Like the previous chapter, it will have a "nuts and bolts" emphasis. Continuing Kirk and Miller's (1986) general description of the four phases of qualitative research; this chapter will turn from planning to observation, analysis, and reporting. The chapter begins with a broad overview from Merton et al. (1956) of researchers' goals throughout the entire interview process. Their summary is particularly useful at this point because it emphasizes issues that bridge the gap between planning and conducting the research.

Observation

Merton et al. (1956) present four broad criteria for the effective focus group interview: It should cover a maximum range of relevant topics, it should provide data that is as specific as possible, it should foster interaction that explores the participants' feelings in some depth, and it should take into account the personal context that participants use in generating their responses to the topic. They summarize these as range, specificity, depth, and personal context.

Under the heading of range, Merton et al. discuss the extent of relevant observations that the participants produce. Successful groups discuss a range of topics that not only covers the issues that researchers already know to be important, but also introduce a set of issues that the researchers had not anticipated. As an example, in the heart attack focus groups we carefully avoided all mentions of the term *risk factor,* and then checked the range of things that participants mentioned against standard medical lists of risk factors. By not cueing them to this concept, we were able to use it to check the range of issues that they discussed and to observe the extent to which their own conceptions of what caused and prevented heart attacks introduced issues that went beyond accepted medical standards.

Merton et al. emphasize specificity to direct the focus group discussions toward concrete and detailed accounts of the participants' experiences. When attitudes and opinions are elicited, it is important to locate the specific bases for these generalizations. Part of the reason that the Merton team emphasized specificity was to meet their goal of evaluating films and other media: They needed to observe the direct sources of positive and negative impressions. A similar argument was presented in Chapter 3 to advocate observations that concentrate on participants' experiences with a topic. An emphasis on experiences allows researchers to apply the principle of specificity in focus groups that operate without external stimuli. When there are no external stimuli to guide the discussion, it is very easy for the participants to drift off into generalities, but this tendency can be counteracted by a continual emphasis on hearing about the participants' personal and vicarious experiences.

Merton et al. emphasize depth in order to ensure the participants' involvement with the material they are discussing. Once again, the problem is with a discussion that allows observation of nothing more than vague generalizations. Depth is more of a problem with discussions that are based on external stimuli, and Merton et al. discuss a variety of techniques for generating observation that have sufficient depth. By comparison, participants naturally become highly involved in discussions of personal experiences and techniques for guaranteeing depth are seldom necessary. Thus the use of experiences generates a level of depth that transfers from individuals to the involvement of the entire group in the discussion. This was also the goal of the techniques developed by Merton et al.

The final criterion for observations that Merton et al. offered was attention to the personal contact from which individual remarks arise— what is it about a particular participant that leads her or him to see things in a particular way? A similar emphasis was also introduced earlier under the heading of perspective. The goal is to obtain observations that give the researcher an understanding of the participants' perspectives on the topic of interest. This personal context may be based on the social roles and categories that a participant occupies, or it may be rooted in individual experience. Either way, the point of doing a group interview is to bring a number of different perspectives into contact. Without the interaction around a researcher-supplied topic, individuals are often safely unaware of their own perspective, and even when they do contemplate their world view, there is not the same effort needed to explain or defend it to someone who sees the world differently. Using focus groups to create such interactions gives the researcher a set of observations that is difficult to obtain through other methods.

Determining the Interview Content

Meeting the broad criteria of Merton et al. (1956) requires attention to the concrete issues of interview content. The goal here is to construct an interview that covers the particular topic at hand while providing observations that satisfy the larger demands of an affective focus group.

The most obvious constraint on interview content is the typical length of a session, between one and two hours. Safe advice would be to set the length at one and a half hours, but tell participants that it will run two hours—this half-hour cushion avoids the disruption of the group dynamics from "early" leavers. Within this time span, it is important to maintain the focus and not explore too many topics. For an unstructured group, this might mean just two broadly stated topic questions. In a more structured group, the limit should probably be four or five, with preplanned probes under each major topic. (It is always possible to begin with a few of very general groups and then follow these with other groups that emphasize more specific elements of the initial findings.)

For higher levels of moderator involvement, it is useful to organize the discussion topics into a guide that the moderator follows in more or less the same order from group to group (Wells, 1974), in much the same way that individual interviewing is organized. The structure that a guide imposes on discussions is valuable both in channeling the group interaction and in making comparisons across groups in the analysis phase of the research. A good guide creates a natural progression across topics with some overlap between the topics—an artificial compartmentalization of the discussion defeats the purpose of using group discussion. An additional value to creating a guide is to ensure consensus among the various members of the research team with regard to which topics are to be covered at what level of detail.

You create a guide by first preparing a full list of the questions you would like to have answered, and then organizing this into an ordered set of topics. Note that you begin with questions, but convert this to a set of summary topics. There are several problems with organizing your actual guide around direct questions (Templeton, 1976): It is a slow-paced and boring approach to group discussion; participants spend so much time interacting with the moderator that they ignore each other; participants have little opportunity to cut off a topic or spontaneously move in an entirely different direction; and, as survey researchers know all too well, people may answer the questions no matter how uninformed or uninvolved they are. For similar reasons, it is also best to commit the outline to memory—if the moderator is forever referring to a printed list of topics, participants will hang back in their discussions, waiting to hear what the research agenda is.

It is also important to take the concept of a guide quite literally, avoiding the tendency to follow your predetermined order of topics in a rigid fashion. This is one of several improper approaches to moderating that Merton et al. (1956) term fallacies, in this case, the fallacy of adhering to fixed questions. Instead, the moderator needs to be free to probe more deeply when necessary, skip over areas that have already been covered, and follow completely new topics if they arise. Your guide should produce *occasional* moderator directions such as, "Let's hold off on that, we'll get to it in a little while," but if such remarks become a frequent feature of the discussions, you need to either revise the guide or apply it less rigidly. With a good guide, and perhaps a little pretesting, you can count on discussion flowing from topic to topic, avoiding Merton et al.'s fallacy of rapid shifts.

The variety of problems encountered in structuring focus groups around direct questions, relying on preprinted lists of topics, and making an overly rigid use of a guide all reinforce the point that even structured interviews should not be moderator-dominated discussions. The role consists of being the moderator of someone else's discussion and should not be that of an interviewer. Also, a moderator who appears to be an expert on the topic will shut off many lines of discussion, and this is a problem that must be dealt with when the topic for the focus group is introduced at the very beginning of the session.

Both high and low moderator involvement sessions begin the same way. In either case, it is important to open the session by introducing the topic in an honest but fairly general fashion. There are two reasons for beginning at the level of generalities. First, participants may not be able to follow a researcher's detailed thinking on a topic. Second, they may be looking for some sense of purpose and direction, and a detailed introduction can lead them to restrict and channel their discussion. A combination of these two can be deadly. This introduction of the topic is typically accompanied by a few ground rules: only one person speaking at a time, not carrying on side conversations among neighbors, encouraging everyone to participate with no one dominating, and so on.

The best introduction is often the honest admission that you are there to learn from them, what Bellenger et al. (1976) term a pose of "incomplete understanding." But do not carry this to the extreme of faking ignorance. Participants are unlikely to be fooled by this, and you also run the risk of hearing a series of lectures from newly appointed experts, rather than an open discussion. Your goal actually is to learn from their greater experience, so express it in those terms. This provides a good justification for retiring from the discussion in low-moderator involvement sessions, and a good basis for probing even the most seemingly obvious of statements in high-moderator involvement sessions. Axelrod (1975b: 10) notes that, "Almost anyone will respond to someone who wants to hear her problems, listen to her experiences, and find out how she thinks and feels. That kind of promise brings a respondent to a session with the essential eagerness."

The group discussion itself typically begins with each participant making an individual, uninterrupted statement, often of an autobiographical nature. This procedure serves as a good icebreaker by not only getting everyone to speak at least once, but by providing both the moderator and the other participants with some basic information about everyone. In low-moderator involvement groups, the participants can be instructed to use this introductory information to draw others into the discussion, while more highly involved moderators can do this themselves. Opening statements also help in dealing with latecomers: latecomers are a problem in any event, but one easy rule is not to include anyone who arrives after the opening statements have ended and the discussion proper has begun.

A more subtle advantage of getting each person to make an opening statement is that it helps to deter "groupthink" (Janis, 1982), that is, the tendency for dissenters to suppress their disagreements in favor of maintaining consensus in the group. Opening statements are a way of getting everyone on record with their different experiences and opinions before a consensus emerges. This process can be reinforced by asking people to take a couple of minutes to make written notes prior to their opening statements: There is something about the process of writing things down that reinforces a person's commitment to contributing them to the group, even in the face of apparent disapproval (Greenbaum, 1987; Templeton, 1987). When an apparent consensus does emerge, the material from opening statements gives other participants and the moderator a basis for probing the strength and the breadth of the consensus.

How one moves from the opening to the body of the discussion will depend, in large part, on the level of moderator involvement. With low levels of moderator involvement, there will be a presentation of an initial topic, followed by a relatively unstructured group discussion that proceeds until the moderator introduces a second topic, and so on. Given the unstructured nature of this discussion, it makes sense to keep the topic very broad. For example, the widowhood focus groups were relatively short (one hour) and consisted of only a single topic, "What sorts of things have made it easier for you and what sorts of things have made it harder?" Allowing for overlaps between topics is illustrated by the focus groups that we conducted on beliefs about heart attacks (Morgan and Spanish, 1985), which lasted about an hour and a half and consisted of two topics: "Who has heart attacks and why?" and "What causes and what prevents heart attacks?" We used a time criterion to divide the discussion between these two topics: If the first half of the discussion ran down to a natural conclusion, then we simply introduced the second topic; if the first half ran over time, the similarity of the second topic allowed us to break into the discussion and redirect it with a minimum of disruption.

Matters are somewhat more complicated in high moderator-involvement sessions and here the use of a guide becomes crucial. Wells (1974) refers to the consistent application of a guide throughout a group discussion as tracking. The goals of tracking are to assure both that all desired topics are pursued and that a clear and consistent order is maintained across sessions. Given these goals, the initial topic that the moderator introduces is meant to spark discussion. Many of the issues that are raised at this point, however, will have to be held off and then reintroduced when the appropriate point in the guide is reached. As spurs to discussion, these initial topics may be very similar to the examples just given for unstructured groups, but in this case discussions of these highly general issues will be relatively brief.

The intent of starting a structured group with a general question is not to get a full answer to this question, but to set up an agenda of topics to be discussed within the limits of a flexible guide. So, after perhaps five minutes of open discussion, the moderator will create an opportunity to introduce the first substantive topic on the guide: "One thing I've heard several people mention is "X"; I wonder what the rest of you have to say about that?" But the goal of tracking requires that other things that were mentioned in the opening discussion be remembered and used to introduce the later topics in the guide: "I recall that some of you mentioned something a little different earlier, and I wonder how things like "Y" fit into the picture?" Of course, the opening discussion is not the only source of material that will have to be remembered and tracked down at later points in the guide.

Because tracking leads the moderator to refer to material that participants raised earlier, it provides a mechanism for moving to the next segment of the guide. This is especially useful when too much emphasis on the researcher's outline, and not enough on the participants' own interests, is stifling the discussion. In this case, tracking allows you to return to material that you know the group is interested in as a basis for further discussion. Not every group is equally interested in every topic in a guide. These problems relate to two more of Merton et al.'s mistakes in moderating the fallacy of arresting reports and the fallacy of forcing topics.

Just as the transition between individual opening statements and actual group discussion provides a clear beginning to the group, it is also a good idea to provide a clear indication of when the session is ending. In low-moderator involvement groups, the simple return of the moderator to the table provides this cue. In high-moderator involvement groups, asking each person to give a final summary statement is a useful technique. A sense that the final statement will not be interrupted or challenged may allow a participant to make a contribution that he or she has been holding back from the open discussion. Some moderators take advantage of this potential new material by letting the discussion continue after the group is supposedly over, with the tape continuing to roll during this more informal exchange. If there is good reason to believe that individuals have not expressed their full opinions, then an additional possibility is to call each participant a day or two after the session for a brief thank-you and the opportunity to express "any other thoughts that may have occurred to you."

The recommendations just given all presume that the researcher is seeking to maintain a relatively high level of comparability across groups, but if the research goals allow or require that groups be noncomparable, then somewhat different procedures apply. In the most common case, material that has been well covered in earlier sessions is given only limited attention in later groups (to assure their similarity to previous groups on these issues) and other topics are pursued in greater detail. For example, a single topic from the earlier discussion guide may expand to become the topic for an entire set of new discussions, with a new guide elevating the various points made in the earlier discussions to the level of topics in the follow-up groups. The original guide may also have had the unintended consequence of limiting the range of discussions, so that a second set of groups are done to explore a different set of related topics. The point here is that maintaining consistency across groups is not a goal in its own right, but one potential means of meeting the goals of the larger research design.

Site Selection and Data Collection

The first consideration in observation is the selection of a site where the research is conducted. The site must balance the needs of participants and the needs of the researcher: There is little use for sites that participants will not come to or where you cannot do your recording.

The most likely alternatives are at the researcher's office, at participants' homes, or at some "neutral site" such as a church or hotel meeting room. It is also increasingly possible to rent facilities for this purpose, at a cost of approximately $200 to $300 per session. These facilities resemble a comfortably furnished group dynamics laboratory, and they are where a majority of marketing focus groups are conducted.

The most basic element of the site is a table for the participants, with circular or rectangular conference tables being the most common options. If the moderator will be present at the table throughout the discussion, then a rectangular table actually represents a U-shaped arrangement of the participants, with the moderator at the head of the table. This arrangement is useful for videotaping, because the camera can be placed behind the moderator to yield a facial view of the participants. In addition, Wells (1974) notes that having the moderator at the head of the table gives some control over individuals' level of participation if the least talkative person is then placed directly across from the moderator and the most talkative ones on either side of the moderator.

The principal means of capturing observations in a focus group is through audio taping, and any choices about physical facilities must be made with tape recording clearly in mind. Because transcripts are the basic data that the research produces, it is absolutely vital that you ensure the quality of the recorded data. Treating recording problems as annoying hassles that get in the way of the "real research" is a dangerous attitude with focus groups. The best research design and the most interesting questions matter little in the face of a blank tape, or even more maddening, one that sounds like a convention of chipmunks at the bottom of a swimming pool. One solution is to get a number of the research team who is knowledgeable about audio and sees these problems as interesting challenges. Failing that, it may be necessary to get an initial consultation on your set-up from a professional (many colleges and universities have an audio-visual department that can provide this service). In any event it is always wise to bring alone a hand-held recorder with fresh batteries in case of emergencies.

Although video taping is a tempting alternative to audio taping, there is really very little to recommend it for this purpose, and several reasons to avoid it. A key difference between audio and video taping is the intrusiveness of the latter. Most people have few problems under-standing the researcher's need for taping to create a record of the discussions, and quickly settle into a discussion that ignores the microphones and recording equipment. By comparison, video set-ups that record full facial and nonverbal detail are hideously complicated— requiring multiple cameras, supplemental lighting, and the absence of windows or other sources of backlighting, and so on. Even with all of this equipment for video, it is important to remember that the actual analysis approach will be based on transcripts, and simple video set-ups (e.g., single camera with built-in mike) have very low quality audio, so you will have to include a full audio set-up even if you do use video.

Given the greater invasion of privacy present with a video record, the research will need to give a clear reason why this kind of information is of value to the project. Marketers do make considerable use of video because they use edited tapes as a major component of their ultimate report to the client. This is not a typical way to present social science research, but if it is a useful format for the presentation of your results, then you will want to consider the expense and effort necessary to produce quality video recordings. One simple but expensive way to do video taping is to rent facilities from a marketing agency.

The most useful purpose for video is in determining who is speaking, and in conversations, who is speaking to whom. With audio taping, such matters are usually tracked by an assistant who makes notes that the transcript typist will later use to identify each speaker (this information is often not obvious from just listening to the tape). Counting on video tapes to provide much more information than this is probably overestimating what can be captured through such means. In particular, even high quality video set-ups will not fully reproduce "group dynamics." As Marshall McCluhan noted, taping has a tendency to cool things down, and although a video may remind a moderator of the emotions that were present around the table, there is no way that it will convey this same sense to someone who was not present during the original discussion.

A different issue is raised by the fact that marketing researchers typically use rooms that contain one-way mirrors, and if you rent a facility that is regularly used for such research, a mirror will almost certainly be present. In marketing, these set-ups allow clients and executives from the advertising agency to observe groups and "get a feel" for the discussions, but it is difficult to imagine parallel needs for covert observation in the typical social science focus group. One possibility is when a project is extremely pressed for time and some members of the research teams cannot wait for transcripts or summary analyses; in that case a mirror would allow them to observe without disrupting the discussions.

For social scientists, the more common means of supplementing observations is through the collection of questionnaires in addition to transcripts. Supplementing transcript data with questionnaires has both disadvantages and advantages. The largest disadvantage is that the two methods are mutually contaminating: doing questionnaires first will direct the group discussion, whereas doing the group first may change attitudes. Also, using questionnaires adds another layer of complexity; it is not a case of getting something for nothing. For example, it is more difficult to handle latecomers when using prequestionnaires: there is no data on one of the participants who is an influence on discussions in the whole group; equivalently, with postquestionnaires, there will be those who need to leave prior to supplying the desired data.

Questionnaires do have some advantages. Getting at least a few background items is a virtual necessity, if only to provide an accurate sense of who is actually participating, e.g., is there an unintentionally limited range on social class. Even in the classic case of focus groups as exploratory research, some marketers (e.g., Rosenstein, 1976) advocate using questionnaires for quantification, both to pretest hypotheses and to provide a safeguard against overly subjective interpretations of the group discussions. Further, in some specialized designs, such as attitude-change studies, pre- and postquestionnaires are a virtual necessity. In any case, it is important to avoid surveylike interpretations of questionnaire data, given the small size and nonrepresentativeness of the sample.

Regardless of whether the data collection includes questionnaires, there should be field notes from the moderator after each session. Experienced fieldworkers can either type or tape their own notes. If the moderator has little experience in social science of fieldwork, another member of the team can collect the data via a debriefing interview immediately after the session. Because they involve interpretation, these notes are, properly speaking, part of the analysis rather than the data collection, but it is wise not to maintain an overly artificial distinction between these aspects of the research. One caveat applies to premature interpretation in high moderator involvement groups: Kennedy (1976) warns that forming premature conclusions can lead the moderator to bias later groups in favor of confirming these expectations. As an antidote he recommends that moderators become as familiar as possible with their own biases, if note taking *explicitly* serves the goal of making expectations apparent, then the moderator can use this self-awareness to limit conscious attempts to confirm his or her biases.

Analysis

The two basic approaches to analyzing focus group data are a strictly qualitative or ethnographic summary and a systematic coding via content analysis. The principal difference is that the ethnographic approach relies more on direct quotation of the group discussions, while the content analysis typically produces numerical descriptions of the data. The present approach is to argue for the validity of both ethnographic and content analysis, although more emphasis will be devoted to content analysis, given the existing coverage of ethnographic approaches in the marketing literature (e.g., Templeton, 1987). These are not, however, conflicting means of analysis, and there is generally an additional strength that comes from combining the two. Thus a largely ethnographic approach may benefit from a systematic tallying of one or two key topics, while a basically quantitative summary of the data is improved immensely by including quotes that demonstrate the points being made.

In either mode of analysis, it must be recognized that the group is the fundamental unit of analysis, and that the analysis will at least begin in a group-by-group progression. A useful strategy is to begin with a detailed examination of one or two groups, developing hypotheses and coding schemes that can then be applied to the remainder of the groups. Another useful strategy is to have one person examine one set of transcripts, while another concentrates on a different set of discussions. This allows for two processes of discovery in the material. An illustration comes from the work that Margaret Spanish and I did with our groups on heart attack risk factors (Morgan and Spanish, 1985). This paper is particularly useful for this purpose, as it combines elements of the ethnographic approach with a content analysis: While the discussion section of the paper is built around the tabular presentation of how often different risk factors were mentioned, the body of the paper is an ethnographic examination of *how* risk factor information was introduced and discussed in the groups.

As described in Chapter 3, a major topic of the article was how interaction in groups influenced the formation of schematic knowledge about risk factors for heart attacks. To make our case for schema formation through interaction, the body of the paper was about one-third quotations, with the remainder divided between setting the stage for quotations and interpreting what the quotations meant. But where did this material come from, out of nearly 200 pages of transcripts, and how did we choose the material that we actually presented?

In a sense, this question puts the cart before the horse: In order to know what quotes to select, we had to know what points we wanted to illustrate. Some topics were clear to us from our observations of the groups while we conducted the discussions, while other topics emerged from our analysis of the data. For example, from moderating the groups we "knew" that question-asking among the participants had a major influence on their discussions. In essence, we had identified "asking questions" as a code category that we wanted to explore systematically in our data. To do the actual coding associated with questioning, we divided the transcripts and each of us went through half, marking all of the instances of asking questions. At the same time, we also looked for other points in the discussions where there seemed to be an effort to organize existing information, so that each of us was conducting our own separate attempt to develop code categories. Note that this kind of analytic coding is not the same as content analysis, a distinction that will be taken up next.

With regard to asking questions, the material that we found was rich enough to confirm our initial impression that this was an important aspect of how interaction influenced knowledge formation; our coding also provided us with a set of potential quotes to illustrate the dynamics of questioning. With regard to developing new code categories, one of the things that we both noticed was the importance of comparisons among different points of view. Each of us had selected a set of passages to illustrate comparisons, so that we were in essence using quotes to argue for the creation of this new code category. Once we accepted comparisons as a new category, we went back to the transcripts, both confirming its importance and selecting quotations for presentation as part of our argument about how interaction, in the form of comparisons, influenced knowledge about heart attacks.

As this example demonstrates, there is likely to be a cycling back and forth between the raw material in the transcripts and the more abstract determination of what topics will go into the ultimate report. At any one point in an ethnographic analysis such as this, the material in the transcripts is simultaneously serving as a source of potential quotes for confirmed code categories and a source of inspiration for new code categories. This cyclical process for developing hypotheses and coding schemes is a major issue in less structured focus groups, where the topics are not predetermined in the form of a moderator guide, and where discussion of any topic can occur anywhere in any of the transcripts.

When the focus group has been conducted from a moderator guide, the topics in the guide will serve as a practical structure for organizing the topic-by-topic analysis of the discussions. The fact that the guide organizes each group's discussion around the same set of topics in the same order is a strong point in its favor during the analysis, because it facilitates the comparison of the groups. Even so, no guide should be so rigid that it guarantees that all discussion of a certain topic occurs at one and only one point in each discussion. The result is that any analysis of focus group transcripts involves a large amount of flipping from page to page, both within a single transcript and between different groups.

The complexity of comparing discussions across several groups has led to several techniques for facilitating this comparison, including what Wells (1974) terms the "scissor and sort" or "long couch, short hall" approach. The basic idea is that relevant passages in each transcript are marked and copied, then cut apart and sorted, typically on some long flat surface such as a couch seat or hall floor. A more recently developed alternative is the use of multiple shades of colored highlighter. At this point, the state of the art involves computer-assisted coding. Even basic word processing programs now include the kind of search functions that enable researchers to locate quickly the points at which a given topic is discussed.

More advanced computer programs that act as textual data bases allow the researcher to mark each instance of a topic or other point of interest and to code it according to possibly multiple attributes. While such functions are helpful for an ethnographic analysis of the data, they are especially useful in the course of a systematic content analysis. By generating reports of where and how often various codes occur, these programs allow the researcher to automate the process of counting instances of code categories within and across transcripts. (For a more detailed discussion of computerized content analysis, see Weber, 1985.)

In practical terms, what does a content analysis look like? Whether the coding is done with pencil and paper or on a computer, the key is to locate a set of items that can be systematically counted. For example, in contrast to the broad, analytic code categories that characterized the ethnographic phase of the work that Spanish and I did on heart attacks, our content analysis of these materials hinged on the tallying of mentions of very specific risk factors. By a "mention," we meant any discussion of a specific risk factor; in the following passage the coded mentions are in brackets.

> I think there's a lot of cases where you get this calm, cool, collected person who has got the whole world's problems stuffed inside their bodies, worrying constantly, [*building up tremendous stresses*] that no one else is aware of. And the wife of the guy who drops over at work says, "He's never been excited a day in his life," interested—aggressive is much too strong a word. But at the same time, when someone says, "Hey, the furnace you just built isn't worth a damn," and you say, "Well, there are a couple things wrong with it, blah, blah, blah . . ." And apparently, what has been going on for these X number of years was he just took and ate himself, ate his pump out by worrying about it, and why he didn't have an ulcer—my folk wisdom says he should have had an ulcer before he dropped over of a heart attack. But maybe not, maybe his approach to his pump, as good as it must have been, as an active adult all that sort of stuff, was just as damaging as the [*drinking*]/[*smoking*], smoking/[*eating*] combination. My folk wisdom separates them into two groups.

This segment shows some of the practical difficulties involved in coding decisions: For example, is "ate his pump out by worrying" a metaphorical reference to stress or a literal reference to overeating as a result of the stress, or, does the reference, near the end, to being "an active adult" mean exercise? Not shown in this transcript segment are the actual code categories that we associated with the bracketed mentions. We ultimately reported our risk factors according to 17 separate code categories, but we used considerably more in our actual coding; the many smaller categories in the initial coding system were collapsed into the final, reported system. One reason for this approach is an inability to predict in advance which categories will be too small to stand alone; prematurely collapsing means that potentially important distinctions are lost without extensive recoding. Another reason is to provide evidence that some things are in fact seldom mentioned: in this case, we coded all instances of going to doctors for check-ups as instances of reducing risk by prevention, but we found only one such mention and this for a person who refused to go to a doctor for his chest pains! Having gone to the effort of coding the absence of mentions of doctors put us in a strong position with regard to making assertions about how lay people saw the doctor's role in reducing risk.

This passage also demonstrates quite clearly that "mentions" can be brief (e.g., drinking, smoking, and eating), or quite extensive (e.g., stress). In this content analysis, we reported simple counts and did not attempt to weight mentions in any way. Instead, we called attention to this issue by distinguishing between what the participants found to be interesting versus what they found to be important (see Chapter 3); in other words, we treated this as a substantive issue, rather than strictly methodological problem. It would, of course, be possible to orient the coding system to something more than strict counts. Here, a likely approach would be to first report the proportion of the transcripts that was in fact dedicated to risk factors, and then to subdivide this according to the percentage of all discussions of risk factors that was devoted to stress or smoking or drinking, and so on.

The question of whether or not to do any form of systematic content analysis with focus group data is controversial, and many marketing approaches deny all uses of counting: "Numbers do not belong in qualitative study at any time . . ." (Axelrod, 1975a: 7). But it is important to realize that this advice is largely due to the overly strict separation that marketers maintain between qualitative and quantitative research, with the former too often serving solely as a preliminary exploration for the latter. Some quantitative possibilities are both obvious and basic. If one were to conduct discussions of the same topic with distinctively different groups, say separate groups of husbands and wives, then there would be good reason to compare how frequently different aspects of the topic were mentioned in the two different sets of groups.

One common argument against using numbers in the marketing literature is that collecting data in groups violates the assumptions of independence in significance tests. This argument is a clear overstatement if it is used to deny the possibility of using descriptive statistics to analyze focus groups. In my own work, I typically present simple counts from transcripts of focus group data without performing any statistical tests. As always, the issue is the research question that motivates the analysis, and those who can answer their research questions without performing elaborate statistical tests on them should feel well justified in doing so—no appeals to imagined statistical bogeymen are necessary.

Tests of inference take us beyond the use of descriptive statistics. Certainly the prescription of such tests on the basis of violations of assumptions in focus groups has been overstated. The mere collection of observations in groups does not violate any statistical laws; it simply requires proper allowances (e.g., "nested design") for the grouped data, a topic that is well covered in statistical applications to social psychological experimental designs involving group discussion. In the example involving separate groups of husbands and wives, this would allow for a test of whether a given topic was mentioned more frequently in one set of groups than in the other. There are, however, real problems that result from the fact that the data are created in groups, rather than merely collected in them, as each individual may make multiple contributions of the discussion of any given issue in any given group. Those whose research questions require performing inferential tests on focus group data should consult with an expert in experimental design and analysis *prior* to entering the field.

To a large extent, a confusion between the qualitative collection of data and the qualitative analysis of data (Bartos, 1986) is responsible for the debate about using numbers in interpreting focus groups. There is no question that focus groups represent a qualitative means of collecting data, but at this point in the development of social science approaches to focus groups, the place of quantitative analysis remains an open issue. In any event, we would do well to ignore the received wisdom from marketing research in this regard. Focus groups will always remain a qualitative technique for generating data, regardless of how the data are handled. Further, those who rightly argue for the advantages of a qualitative analysis of data that are qualitatively generated should feel secure enough in their own approach to pursue it without rigidly denying the additional possibility of quantitative analyses on the same data.

Reporting

The similarity between focus groups and other qualitative methods is most apparent when it comes to reporting the results of the research. As with other qualitative means of data collection, there are no hard and fast rules when it comes to reporting results. In large part, the format will reflect earlier decisions—according to Becker (1986), by the time the social scientist sits down to write, most of the big choices about how to portray the research have already been made during the course of the research itself. With focus groups, these choices include whether the research was exploratory or hypothesis testing, whether the level of moderator involvement was intended to produce structured or unstructured discussions, and whether the analyses relied on ethnographic or numerical summaries of the data.

Unfortunately, there is not much written on how to report focus groups, and marketers contribute little in this area, as they typically report their conclusions directly to a client, rather than publishing their results as research. One set of useful models for writing up the results of focus group research comes from other qualitative methods. In particular, groups that are based on more structured observation present many of the same issues as reporting on individual interviewing. Because of the use of the interview guide, each discussion covers more or less the same topics in more or less the same order, and the summarization of these topics will be the main business of the report. By comparison, the unstructured nature of more exploratory observation presents many of the same issues as reporting on participant observation. Because participants are free to bring up whatever topics they choose, the observer ends up with more possible topics for analyses than could ever be covered in sufficient detail in a single report. (For a social science example of using a guide in reporting results, Knodel et al., 1987, provide the guide for their earlier studies in an appendix.)

Similar models are available for using quotes and counts to provide evidence, depending on the approach selected for analyzing the data. In the more ethnographic approach, there must be a balance between the direct quotation of the participants and the summarization of their discussions. Too much quotation gives the report a chaotic stream-of-consciousness flavor, while too much summarization is not only dry but also deprives the reader of even the indirect contact with participants available through their verbatim statements of their perspectives. When using content analysis, it is best to use a few relatively simple tables, probably no more than four in an article-length presentation. The goal of the tables is to summarize basic information related to the research enterprise, and each table should represent a major topic in the discussion.

Whatever approach is taken, trying to cover too many topics in too much detail will only confuse the reader. Focus groups are no different than other qualitative methods in this regard: There is a perceptual tension between the richness of the data and the remoteness of the reader from the sources of the data. Reducing this remoteness is almost always a goal of qualitative research, but this is best done through a report that clearly distinguishes which topics are most important and concentrates on a thorough portrayal of only what is most important.

Summing Up

Much of the material in this and the previous chapter has, of necessity, concentrated on technical matters and the choice between alternate versions of the focus group technique. Like any truly useful method of data collection, focus groups have the flexibility to provide researchers with a range of options to respond to a range of circumstances. But appropriate choices among these options require an understanding of the more technical aspects of focus groups. If this presentation has met its goal, the reader will have not only a mastery of the nuts and bolts of focus groups, but also a sense of *why* the issues raised here are critical concerns in planning, conducting, and analyzing focus group research.

While the need to master the nuts and bolts cannot be denied, it is also important not to lose track of the larger issues that influence choices among these options. In particular, the theme that practical decisions depend on larger research goals has appeared several times throughout this discussion. For example, research that explores previously uncharted territory is likely to require a different format from research that decides among well-established competing hypotheses. Certainly one must possess a mastery of the technical aspects of focus groups in order to make such decisions, but that mastery is not an end in itself. Ultimately, the choices that are made depend on the goals that must be served.

6. ADDITIONAL POSSIBILITIES

The future development of focus groups in the social sciences offers many opportunities, thanks to the newness of technique. The key to extending the uses of focus groups is to think in terms of research design. It is certainly possible to design research that consists of only a set of self-contained focus groups and nothing more—this is what much of the qualitative research in marketing looks like, and it may well become the most common application of focus groups in the social sciences as well. Most of the more complex designs presented here involve multiple types of focus groups; it is this systematic variation across groups that is the key to research design with focus groups.

One important set of more complex designs has already been covered: those that combine focus groups and other research methods in the same research project. This chapter will concentrate on research designs that are based solely on focus groups. A word of warning is, however, in order: as noted at several points in the previous chapters, social scientists have yet to explore the boundaries of focus group research. Consequently, many of the ideas that follow remain untried at present and are best approached as suggestions for extending the focus group technique.

Comparative Designs

Two fundamental comparisons across a set of focus groups are who attends and what they discuss. With regard to the latter, it is possible to design a research program based on varying the questions asked in the groups. In its simplest form, this would involve no more than altering the order in which the same questions were asked. Question ordering can be a sensitive issue in any form of interviewing, but the goal in varying questions for design purposes is to go beyond methodological issues to create structured comparisons between groups that discuss variant forms of the same topic. An example would be to expand the heart attack risk factor focus groups, where we originally combined the discussion of things that cause and things that prevent heart attacks. By having one set of groups solely devoted to things that cause heart attacks and another solely to things that prevent them, it would be possible to observe whether the interest and importance attached to risk factors varies between these two different approaches to the same underlying topic.

A potentially more powerful set of design possibilities come from systematically varying the composition of groups. A good example of this kind of research is Knodel's focus groups with different generations of Thais to compare their views on family size and family planning (Knodel et al., 1987). As it happens, Knodel found broad agreement between the two generations, with both agreeing that small family sizes were desirable for members of the younger generation; however, their key point is that this similarity could not have been demonstrated without a systematic comparison. Other suggestions from earlier chapters include separate groups of men and women or husbands and wives. As an alternative to these role- or status-based means of selection, Levy (1979) suggests using comparative focus groups to get the opinions of individuals who fall at various points along the continuum of opinion on an issue. This can be accomplished by asking relevant screening questions during recruitment and creating sets of groups that each consist of individuals with similar opinions.

A related suggestion is to take advantage of issues of homogeneity and heterogeneity in groups by running a two-step research program in which some sessions mix different types of participants and other sessions separate them by type. Templeton (1987) suggests beginning with an exploratory phase when groups are as heterogeneous as possible, and using the outcomes of these discussions to determine the categories of participants for a second set of more homogeneous groups. Another alternative, however, would be to move from more homogeneous to more heterogeneous groups: When the relevant subgroups of participants are known in advance, it may make more sense to begin by understanding the experiences and perspectives of each group before observing the dynamics of interaction between them. Note, however, that designs that compare discussions within separate categories and discussions that combine the categories of participants that can become quite unwieldy: with two categories this means three sets of focus groups.

Templeton provides an example of the differences that occur in running separate versus mixed groups. Following her strategy of beginning with more heterogeneous groups, she first ran a set of marketing groups on hair coloring that combined women who did and did not dye their hair. The result was the kind of hostility that is often warned against in mixed groups, with the women who did not dye their hair expressing a great deal of anger toward any advertising that suggested that gray hair was not attractive to men. When these women were interviewed separately, however, they expressed considerably more self-doubt. Given the potential for conflict that this illustration provides, it would be advisable to exercise caution in combining those whose lifestyles do not normally lead them to discuss a topic together.

A different kind of comparison observes changes that occur within single groups. The basic design here is to observe attitude change that is a result of the group discussion, an idea that goes back to Lewin and beyond. Thus in the focus groups on heart attack risk factors, we asked participants to complete pre- and postquestionnaires that measured whether they felt that most individuals were or were not responsible for causing their own heart attacks. In unpublished analyses, Spanish found that those who initially blamed individuals decreased this tendency, while those who did not blame individuals retained this belief throughout. Qualitative examination of the focus groups transcripts shows that such simplistic explanations are increasingly questioned as discussion proceeds and the complexity of the causes of heart attacks becomes evident.

Multistage Groups

A different kind of variation across groups occurs when participants are brought back for more than one group. In this case, the comparison is between the earlier and later sessions. The most basic version of this design has the same groups meet together several times. Kaden (1977) advocates this kind of design, asking how much a first conversation among strangers really reveals. Just as survey respondents can provide some form of an answer to just about any question, so too can participants in the typical self-contained focus group find a way to discuss just about any topic. This changes, however, as the group members get to know each other and a sense of rapport is built. In second and later groups, there is much less use for moderator guides or explicit self-management techniques, as these groups take on a life of their own. Kaden even suggests that it is possible to ask participants in such continuing groups to pursue assignments between the group meetings and then use these assignments as the basis for the next set of discussions.

Another kind of multistage group can be created in designs that bring back participants from several different earlier groups in what can be termed "second-order" groups. Mixing participants from different previous groups naturally leads to a comparison of the discussion in the several original groups, and it may be wise to include no more than one member from each of the prior discussions. We ran such a second-order group with participants from the heart attack risk factors groups, first asking each person to provide a brief summary of what was discussed in his or her group, and then leaving the rest of the discussion unstructured. What we learned was that the returning students who served as our participants were more interested in stress than heart attacks, and that our preferred topic was almost submerged in a general discussion of stress and coping. Rather than despairing, we began to explore the possibilities of a new research project based on the exploration of "folk beliefs" about stress.

As the example shows, running second-order groups in a relatively unstructured fashion allows the researcher to see which topics continue to be of interest to the participants. Based on this, it could be especially useful to run such a group with low moderator involvement as a follow-up to a set of highly structured groups. Nor is there any reason to stop at second-order groups: Provided that sufficient participants were available, participants from second-order groups could be mixed together to form third-order groups, and so on.

Goldman (1962) describes yet another form of multistage group, based on mixing prior participants with new participants. In his study, an initial group of participants met together several times to discuss their feelings about some radically new designs for appliances. Over the course of their several discussions, the initially negative reactions of these participants became substantially more positive. To see whether this enthusiasm was transferable, Goldman then asked the continuing participants to meet with a set of people who had never seen the new designs before. In this mixed meeting, the continuing participants reverted to their earlier skepticism, and consequently the redesign project was dropped. Goldman suggests that this design comes closer to duplicating interaction in natural contexts, where opinions must first be formed, then communicated and defended.

Summing Up

Goldman's argument about the enhanced realism of mixing continuing and new participants could be extended to other designs with multistage focus groups and to comparative designs as well. Ultimately, however, it is not the extent to which such research designs mimic the real world that determines their ultimate value; rather, it is the ability of these designs to answer research questions. As the material in this chapter has demonstrated, the existing applications for focus groups have only scratched the surface of the possible designs.

The more elaborate research designs in this chapter are yet another demonstration that focus groups are not limited to preliminary and exploratory purposes. Although the ability to generate hypotheses is frequently listed as the chief virtue of focus groups, the argument here is that with appropriate designs they are well suited to hypothesis testing. Still, there is nothing inherently superior about a complex as opposed to a simple research design, unless it truly does offer a better way to address the fundamental questions in the research.

7. CONCLUSIONS

The contribution of focus groups to social science research is, at present, more potential than real. Despite their initial introduction by sociologists and despite 30 years of experience in marketing research, focus groups in the social sciences are still at an early stage in their development. In looking forward to the future of focus groups as a research method in the social sciences, I will examine their potential location within a division of labor among existing methods. Thus it makes sense to consider two other major interest groups: those who practice other qualitative methods in the social sciences and those who conduct focus groups in marketing research.

My basic premise is that it would be unrealistic to expect focus groups to become a widespread research technique in the social sciences based solely on their merits. Such merits are a necessary, but not sufficient, condition for the adoption of focus groups. Although I believe that the previous chapters have made a strong case for focus groups, the realist in me recognizes that the existing choices among social science methods are well institutionalized. Any new method must be considered in terms of its location within this existing structure. Seen in this light, the ability of focus groups to carve out a niche depends in large part upon their relationship to methods that already hold established positions.

One potential future for focus groups in the social sciences derives from their association with quantitative methods. Indeed, in conversations with my colleagues, it seems that survey researchers are the one group who are most aware of and interested in focus groups. As I argued in Chapter 3, focus groups have much to offer survey research, but it is less clear what survey research can offer to focus groups. What I fear is achieving a certain legitimacy through association with a widely accepted method, but at the expense of focus groups not being taken seriously as a self-contained method of data collection. To the extent that focus groups are seen only as a useful addition to other primary methods of data collection, they will never reach their full potential.

The obvious alternative is to emphasize the place of focus groups within qualitative methods. As I noted in Chapter 2, I am optimistic about the ability of focus groups to establish a unique position within the existing array of methods for gathering qualitative data in the social sciences. This optimism is based on the ability of focus groups to fit within the existing division of labor among qualitative methods. A one-sentence summary of the relationship between focus groups and other qualitative methods would be: Focus groups add to, rather than replace, other qualitative methods.

The relationship between focus groups and other qualitative methods goes beyond peaceful coexistence, however. If we are to expand our horizons to include focus groups as a routine option, it will most likely happen through their adoption by those who already have a solid background in qualitative research. This is partly because other uses of focus groups are best understood in comparison to other qualitative techniques, and partly because the analysis of focus group data will be most comfortable for those who already have experience with this process. Practitioners of other qualitative techniques thus constitute a crucial constituency for the future of focus groups.

The outlook for the relationship between marketing and social science applications of focus groups is less sanguine. In part this is because of the differences between the two fields. For marketing research, the research environment outside of focus groups consists almost entirely of quantitative methods, while social scientists can rely on an active tradition of qualitative methods. The audience for marketing research is a bill-paying client, while social scientists address their colleagues in the form of a field of studies or a discipline. And, in marketing, the pragmatic pursuit of increased sales is the overwhelming goal, while social scientists pursue such nebulous goals as "increased understanding."

There is, however, another reason for pessimism about the reception from marketers for social science approaches to focus groups. This is based on the extent to which a specific approach to focus groups has become institutionalized within marketing research, so that those who operate outside the established guidelines are likely to receive the response: "What you're doing is interesting, but it isn't focus groups." This is what Linda Kaboolian and William Gamson (1983) heard when they presented research that they termed focus groups to an audience that included marketers. The problem? Their groups were too small—3 to 5 instead of 6 to 12. Their groups were built around acquaintance-ship—relying on a focal individual to recruit his or her friends as the participants, rather than hiring a firm that specialized in the recruitment of groups of strangers. And, their groups were too informal—meeting in the focal person's house, rather than at a specialized facility.

Partially as a result of this experience, Kaboolian and Gamson now label their research method *peer group conversations*. Only time will tell whether this relabeling is well-advised or overly sensitive ("A rose by any other name . . .?"), but other social scientists who call their research focus groups may have to be prepared for the charge from marketers that what they are doing "isn't focus groups." My response would be that what we are doing may not be good marketing research, but it most certainly is focus groups. I have argued throughout this book that social scientists will have to work hard to adapt the focus group technique to our purposes. This work is vital if focus groups are to be useful in answering our research questions, but there is no reason to expect that those who do marketing research focus groups will thank us for fixing what is not, for their purposes, broken.

In making the case for social science's adoption of focus groups, I have done my best not to overstate the case. There are always short-term advantages to extravagant claims, if only to overcome the inertia that is associated with learning a new technique. Instead, I have chosen to avoid the long-run disappointment that comes from unrealistic expectations. Focus groups are a valuable tool, not a panacea, and they will have to prove themselves on their own merits, although it should be obvious that they cannot do so if they are not given the chance.

Ultimately focus groups will be judged against one unavoidable criterion: Do they provide an improved ability to answer research questions? The promise that any new method offers to the practicing researcher is a further opportunity to match appropriate techniques to research questions, and I believe that focus groups will indeed provide better answers to some of our existing questions. There is an additional criterion, however, that is especially relevant to qualitative methods, and I believe that focus groups will also do what any successful qualitative technique must do: lead us to ask better questions, based on our contacts with the experiences and perspectives of those who participate in our research. As an addition to the existing range of qualitative techniques, focus groups offer an opportunity for growth in an already vigorous field.

Suggestions for Further Reading

The social scientist who wishes to train as a focus groups researcher will find that few of the existing resources have been written with this goal in mind. Each of the following books can contribute to the goal, but it will be up to the reader to read between the lines.

The Focused Interview, by Robert K. Merton, Marjorie Fiske, and Patricia Kendall. Given the authorship, it is hardly surprising that there is still a great deal of insight to be found here. The examples based on World War II training and propaganda films do give the material a dated feeling, but the practical advice on how to manage group interviews is just as useful now as it was then. Its greatest limitation is the continual reliance on the presentation of these films as stimulus materials for the subsequent discussions.

Focus Group Interviews, by James B. Higginbotham and Keith K. Cox. For many years this collection of readings was the only available source on focus groups. After 10 years, it is definitely beginning to show its age, with too many of the entries selected for their recency (at that time) rather than their lasting contribution. Its greatest value today is the set of well-known articles it brings together in one place.

The Practical Handbook and Guide to Focus Group Research, by Thomas L. Greenbaum. One of three recent book-length treatments of focus groups, Greenbaum's approach is that of a supplementary text for a course in marketing research. Within the limits of this goal, the coverage of the material is good, and social scientists wishing to expand their understanding of the technique will find it of interest; a discussion of focus groups with children is especially useful.

Focus Groups: A Guide for Marketing & Advertising Professionals, by Jane Farley Templeton. In contrast to Greenbaum's approach, Templeton's book is written largely for those who actually conduct and consume marketing research. The book gives a good picture of the more psychodynamic and motivational approaches to focus groups. Also useful are appendices that present most of the materials that would be generated during a set of focus groups.

The Group Depth Interview: Principles and Practice, by Alfred E. Goldman and Susan Schwartz McDonald. Goldman is one of the leading lights of qualitative research in marketing, and this book reflects his many years of experience in the field. Among the three recent books in marketing, this is the one that is most likely to become the definitive text on focus groups and, although social scientists will need to translate it into their terms, it is as good a place to start as any. Particularly useful are the many examples that deal with focus groups among physicians and similar professionals.

Focus Groups: A Practical Guide for Applied Research, by Richard A. Krueger. At this writing, Krueger's book is the only other sustained treatment of focus groups outside the field of marketing research. The emphasis here is on the application of focus groups to evaluation research, and most social scientists will find this orientation very accessible. Krueger also gives considerably more attention to the topics of analyzing and reporting focus group results than in the equivalent treatments by marketing researchers. The numerous detailed examples will be especially helpful to those who are just getting started in focus groups.

REFERENCES

Advertising Research Foundation (1985) Focus Groups: Issues and Approaches. New York: Author.

Agar, Michael (1986) Speaking of Ethnography. (Sage University Paper, Qualitative Research Methods series, Vol. 2) Beverly Hills, CA: Sage.

Axelrod, Myril D. (1975a) "Marketers get an eyeful when focus groups expose products, ideas, images, and copy, etc. to consumers." Marketing News 8: 6-7. (Also pp. 51-54 in Higginbotham and Cox, 1979)

Axelrod, Myril D. (1975b) "Ten essentials for good qualitative research." Marketing News 8: 10-11. (Also pp. 55-59 in Higginbotham and Cox, 1979)

Bartos, Rena (1986) "Qualitative research: What it is and where it came from." Journal of Advertising Research 26: RC3-RC6.

Becker, Howard S. (1958) "Problems of inference and proof in participant observation." American Sociological Review 23: 652-660.

Becker, Howard S. (1986) Writing for Social Scientists. Chicago: University of Chicago Press.

Bellenger, Danny N., Kenneth L. Bernhardt, and Jac L. Goldstucker (1976) "Qualitative research techniques: focus group interviews," pp. 7-28 in Danny N. Bellenger, Kenneth L. Bernhardt, and Jac L. Goldstucker (eds.) Qualitative Research in Marketing. Chicago: American Marketing Association. (Also pp. 13-34 in Higginbotham and Cox, 1979)

Calder, Bobby Jo (1977) "Focus groups and the nature of qualitative marketing research." Journal of Marketing Research 14: 353-364.

Converse, Jean M. and Stanley Presser (1986) Survey Questions: Handcrafting the Standardized Questionnaire. (Sage University Paper, Quantitative Research Methods series, Vol. 63) Beverly Hills, CA: Sage.

Denzin, Norman K. (1978) The Research Act: A Theoretical Introduction to Sociological Methods (2nd ed.). New York: McGraw-Hill.

Fern, Edward F. (1982) "The use of focus groups for idea generation: the effects of group size, acquaintanceship, and moderator on response quantity and quality." Journal of Marketing Research 19: 1-13.

Fern, Edward F. (1983) "Focus groups: a review of some contradictory evidence, implications, and suggestions for future research." Advances in Consumer Research 10: 121-126.

Fielding, Nigel G. and Jane L. Fielding (1986) Linking Data. (Sage University Paper, Qualitative Research Methods series, Vol. 4) Beverly Hills, CA: Sage.

Glaser, Barney G. and Anselm L. Strauss (1967) The Discovery of Grounded Theory. Chicago: Aldine.

Goffman, Erving (1981) Forms of Talk. Philadelphia: University of Pennsylvania Press.

Goldman, Alfred E. (1962) "The group depth interview." Journal of Marketing 26: 61-68. (Also pp. 43-50 in Higginbotham and Cox, 1979)

82

Goldman, Alfred E. and Susan S. McDonald (1987) The Group Depth Interview: Principles and Practices. Englewood Cliffs, NJ: Prentice-Hall.

Greenbaum, Thomas L. (1987) The Practical Handbook and Guide to Focus Group Research. Lexington, MA: Lexington Books.

Gubrium, Jaber F. (1987) Oldtimers and Alzheimer's: The Descriptive Organization of Senility. Greenwich, CT: JAI Press.

Hannah, Maggie (1978) "A perspective in focus groups." Viewpoints 18: 4-8. (Also pp. 75-78 in Higginbotham and Cox, 1979)

Higginbotham, James B. and Keith K. Cox [eds.] (1979) Focus Group Interviews: A Reader. Chicago: American Marketing Association.

Hochschild, Arlie R. (1983) The Managed Heart: Commercialization of Human Feeling. Berkeley, CA: University of California Press.

Ingersoll, Fern and Jasper Ingersoll (1987) "Both a borrower and a lender be: ethnography, oral history, and grounded theory." Oral History Review 15: 81-102.

Janis, Irving L. (1982) Groupthink (2nd ed.). Boston: Houghton-Mifflin.

Kaboolian, Linda and William A. Gamson (1983) "New strategies for the use of focus groups for social science and survey research." Presented at the meetings of the American Association for Public Opinion Research.

Kaden, Robert J. (1977) "Incomplete use keeps focus groups from producing optimum results." Marketing News 11: 4. (Also pp. 120-121 in Higginbotham and Cox, 1979)

Kennedy, Frank (1976) "The focused group interview and moderator bias." Marketing Review 31: 19-21. (Also pp. 88-91 in Higginbotham and Cox, 1979)

Kirk, Jerome and Marc L. Miller (1986) Reliability and Validity of Qualitative Research. (Sage University Paper, Qualitative Research Methods series, Vol. 1) Beverly Hills, CA: Sage.

Knodel, John, Apichat Chamratrithirong, and Nibhon Debavalya (1987) Thailand's Reproductive Revolution: Rapid Fertility Decline in a Third-World Setting. Madison, WI: University of Wisconsin Press.

Knodel, John, Napaporn Havanon, and Anthony Pramualratana (1984) "Fertility transition in Thailand: a qualitative analysis." Population and Development Review 10: 297-328.

Krueger, Richard A. (1988) Focus Groups: A Practical Guide for Applied Research. Newbury Park, CA: Sage.

Langer, Judith (1978) "Clients: check qualitative researcher's personal traits to get more; qualitative researchers: enter entire marketing process to give more." Marketing News 12: 10-12. (Also pp. 85-87 in Higginbotham and Cox, 1979)

Latane, Bibb, Kipling Williams, and Stephen G. Harkins (1979) "Many hands make light work: the causes and consequences of social loafing." Journal of Experimental Social Psychology 37: 822-32.

Lazarsfeld, Paul F. (1972) Qualitative Analysis: Historical and Critical Essays. Boston: Allyn and Bacon.

Levy, Sidney J. (1979) "Focus group interviewing," pp. 34-42 in James B. Higginbotham and Keith K. Cox (eds.) Focus Group Interviews: A Reader. Chicago: American Marketing Association.

Merton, Robert K. (1987) "The focused interview and focus groups: continuities and discontinuities." Public Opinion Quarterly 51: 550-556.

Merton, Robert K., Marjorie Fiske, and Patricia L. Kendall (1956) The Focused interview. Glencoe, IL: Free Press.

Merton, Robert K. and Patricia L. Kendall (1946) "The focused interview." American Journal of Sociology 51: 541-557.

Merton, Robert K., George G. Reader, and Patricia L. Kendall (1957) The Student Physician. Cambridge, MA: Harvard University Press.

Moran, William T. (1986) "The science of qualitative research." Journal of Advertising Research 26: RC16-RC19.

Morgan, David L. (1986) "Personal relationships as an interface between social networks and social cognitions." Journal of Social and Personal Relationships 3: 403-422.

Morgan, David L. (forthcoming) "Adjusting to widowhood: do social networks really make it easier?" Gerontologist.

Morgan, David L. and Margaret T. Spanish (1984) "Focus groups: a new tool for qualitative research." Qualitative Sociology 7: 253-270.

Morgan, David L. and Margaret T. Spanish (1985) "Social interaction and the cognitive organisation of health-relevant behavior." Sociology of Health and Illness 7: 401-422.

Morgan, David L. and Margaret T. Spanish (1987) "Post-crisis social psychology: an integration of role theory and social cognition." Presented at the meetings of the Pacific Sociological Association.

Pramualratana, Anthony, Napaporn Havanon, and John Knodel (1985) "Exploring the normative age at marriage in Thailand: an example from focus group research." Journal of Marriage and the Family 47: 203-210.

Punch, Maurice (1986) Politics and Ethics of Fieldwork. (Sage University Paper, Qualitative Research Methods series, Vol. 3) Beverly Hills, CA: Sage.

Rook, Karen S. (1987) "Reciprocity of social exchange and social satisfaction among older women." Journal of Personality and Social Psychology 52: 145-154.

Rosenstein, Alvin J. (1976) "Quantitative—yes, quantitative—applications for the focus group, or what do you mean you've never heard of 'multivariate focus groups?'" Marketing News 9: 8. (Also pp. 118-119 in Higginbotham and Cox, 1979)

Rossi, Peter H., James D. Wright, and Andy B. Anderson [eds.] (1983) Handbook of Survey Research. New York: Academic Press.

Speedling, Edward (1982) Heart Attack. New York: Methuen.

Taylor, Shelley E. and Susan T. Fiske (1981) "Getting inside the head: methodologies for process analysis in attribution and social cognition," pp. 459-524 in John H. Harvey, William Ickes, and Robert F. Kidd (eds.) New Directions in Attribution Research, Vol. 3. Hillsdale, NJ: Lawrence Erlbaum.

Templeton, Jane F. (1976) "Research as giraffe: an identity crisis." Advances in Consumer Research 4: 442-446. (Also pp. 70-74 in Higginbotham and Cox, 1979)

Templeton, Jane F. (1987) Focus Groups: A Guide for Marketing & Advertising Professionals. Chicago: Probus.

Thorne, Barrie and Nancy Henley [eds.] (1975) Language and Sex: Difference and Dominance. Rowley, MA: Newbury House.

Thurstone, L. L. and E. J. Chave (1929) The Measurement of Attitude. Chicago: University of Chicago Press.

Weber, Robert (1985) Basic Content Analysis. (Sage University Paper, Quantitative Research Methods series, Vol. 49) Beverly Hills, CA: Sage.

Welch, Joe L. (1985) "Researching marketing problems and opportunities with focus groups." Industrial Marketing Management 14: 245-253.

Wells, William D. (1974) "Group interviewing," pp. 133-146 in Robert Ferber (ed.) Handbook of Marketing Research. New York: McGraw-Hill. (Also pp. 2-12 in Higginbotham and Cox, 1979)

ABOUT THE AUTHOR

DAVID L. MORGAN received his Ph.D. in sociology from the University of Michigan and did postdoctoral work at Indiana University. He is an Assistant Professor in the Institute on Aging and Department of Urban Studies at Portland State University. His research interests center on the role that social networks and social cognitions play in adult socialization. Under the heading of role transitions in later life, he has studied retirement communities, nursing homes, widowhood, knowledge about risk factors for heart attacks, and caregiving for elderly family members.

NOTES

NOTES

NOTES